Recipes from the Old South

Recipes

from the

Old South

by Martha Meade

Bramhall House • New York

This edition is published by Bramhall House,
a division of Clarkson N. Potter, Inc.,
by arrangement with Holt, Rinehart and Winston

g   h

Library of Congress Catalog Card
Number: 61-8621

Designer: Ernst Reichl

Printed in the United States of America

Foreword

To those who have lived in, or visited—or even read about—that part of the United States known as "the South," the words "Southern cooking" mean *good food*. I hope every one of them will like this collection of my own favorite family recipes. It was begun when I was first a career girl away from my Virginia home. Cooking was, and is, my favorite hobby, and I wanted the recipes I had grown up with to be readily available to one and all.

There has been great improvement in methods of preparation since these old formulas were first recorded. As an illustration, I cite the recipe I use for Peach Pickle as compared to the family-famous one used at home. The original called for heating the syrup and pouring it over the peaches for nine successive mornings. Thanks to the superiority of our present-day mixed pickling spices over the one or two spices in the "boil-for-nine-mornings" recipe, this modern one is tops.

As to seasonings, brown sugar, onion, and tabasco are definitely favorites of mine. All three give a great lift to food. I like hot flavors, so tabasco appears in many recipes. I use it rather than red pepper in all but the following three: I still like to see grains of red pepper in mayonnaise, and to use a small snip of a hot red pepper pod in both my old-fashioned roast chicken and snap beans long cooked with a ham bone. In other cases tabasco is much more convenient to use and there is no danger of deterioration.

Aside from actual family recipes, I have collected familiar ones which have some slightly different twist. Although the unusual appeals to me, my aim has been to make available good recipes for the good food served in Southern homes.

Contents

Appetizers 3

Sandwiches 15

Breads (Quick) 17

Breads (Yeast) 27

Soups 37

Meats 45

Egg and Cheese Dishes 77

Sea Foods 83

Vegetables 91

Salads and Salad Dressings 107

Cakes and Cookies (and Cake Frostings) 117

Desserts 137

Beverages 153

Pickles and Relishes 159

Jams and Jellies, Marmalades and Preserves 165

Confectioneries 171

Index 177

Recipes from the Old South

Appetizers

Bacon Biscuit Balls

1 pound sliced bacon
4 tablespoons chopped green
   pepper
3 tablespoons chopped fresh
   mushrooms
1½ cups flour

2 teaspoons baking powder
¼ teaspoon dry mustard
1 egg, beaten
½ cup milk
¼ cup bacon drippings

Fry bacon until crisp. Save the drippings. Snip bacon into small pieces and combine with green pepper and mushrooms. Sift together flour, baking powder, and dry mustard. Mix bacon and vegetables with flour. Add combined egg, milk, and bacon drippings. Stir the mixture with a fork. Drop by teaspoonfuls onto greased cooky sheet. Bake in a hot (425-degree) oven about 8 minutes. Serve on wooden picks with any highly seasoned dip.

Stuffed Beets

6 cooked beets, very small
¼ cup French dressing
1 hard-boiled egg, mashed with
   table fork

2 small sour cucumber pickles,
   finely chopped
¼ teaspoon dry mustard
Salt, pepper, and tabasco to taste

Marinate beets several hours in French dressing. Scoop out part of inside, fill with paste made by mixing remaining ingredients.

Butter Browns

2 teaspoons dry mustard
2 teaspoons Worcestershire sauce
3 tablespoons butter

Dash of tabasco
Crackers

Make paste of mustard and Worcestershire sauce, blend well. Add to butter and beat until creamy. Add tabasco and mix in thoroughly. Spread on thin crackers and brown in moderate (350-degree) oven.

Calcuttas

Soak large prunes overnight. Dry them and remove stones. Stuff prunes with favorite chutney, roll strip of bacon around each one and fasten with toothpicks. Broil until bacon is crisp and serve hot.

Canapé Spread

3 ounces Roquefort cheese
3 ounces sharp Cheddar cheese
3 ounces cream cheese

2 tablespoons chili sauce
1½ ounces brandy

Blend all ingredients together to form a smooth paste. Season to taste with Worcestershire sauce and tabasco. Serve on crackers or in a bowl surrounded by potato chips to dip in the spread. Or thin with French dressing to make salad dressing for hearts of lettuce.

Celery Cheese Balls

1 cup finely chopped celery
3 ounces cream cheese
1/4 teaspoon salt
2 tablespoons finely chopped
   parsley

Dash white pepper
Dash tabasco
Paprika

Mix together celery, cheese, and seasonings; shape into small balls. Roll in chopped parsley and sprinkle with paprika.

Cheese Apples

8 ounces cream cheese
1/2 cup finely chopped nut meats
1 dozen small pickled onions

Salt, pepper, and tabasco to taste
Paprika
12 cloves

Soften cream cheese; add nut meats, onions, salt, pepper, and tabasco. Mix well. Form into small balls; roll one side in paprika and insert small clove for stem. Makes 12.

Cheese Balls

8 ounces cream cheese
Sherry wine (about 1/4 cup)

1/2 pound (about) chopped almonds or pecans

Blend sherry wine into cream cheese. Shape into small balls and chill. Roll in chopped nuts.

Cheese Biscuits

4 tablespoons flour
6 tablespoons grated Parmesan
   cheese
3 tablespoons vegetable shortening or shortening and butter
   mixed

1 egg yolk
2 teaspoons cold water
Salt and red pepper to taste

Mix flour and cheese; add salt and red pepper. Rub in shortening lightly. Mix egg yolk with water; add enough egg to flour mixture to make stiff paste. Knead until smooth on floured board, then roll out and cut with small cutter. Lay on greased baking sheet and bake in 425-degree oven about 10 minutes. Sharp Cheddar cheese may be substituted for Parmesan.

Cheese Diamonds

2 cups flour, sifted
3 teaspoons baking powder
1 teaspoon salt
¼ cup shortening

1 cup grated sharp Cheddar cheese
⅔ to ¾ cup milk

Sift flour, baking powder, and salt together. Rub in shortening. Add cheese and mix. Add sufficient milk to make a soft dough and blend well. Roll dough one inch thick and cut into diamond-shaped biscuits. Bake in 450-degree oven for 10 or 12 minutes.

Cheese Snappies

1 cup butter
1 pound sharp Cheddar cheese, grated

2 cups flour, sifted
Dash cayenne pepper

Cream butter and cheese together. Add flour and cayenne and mix well. Form into roll about 1½ inches thick. Chill in refrigerator (preferably overnight). Slice into wafers about ½ inch thick. Bake 15 to 20 minutes in a 375-degree oven.

Cheese Spread

1½ pounds sharp Cheddar cheese
¼ teaspoon salt
¾ teaspoon dry mustard
¼ cup chopped parsley
¼ cup chopped onion

2 tablespoons soft butter
Dash of tabasco
Dash of Worcestershire sauce
¼ cup tomato catsup
⅓ cup sherry

Grate cheese, add salt, mustard, parsley, and onion. Work in butter. Add tabasco and Worcestershire sauce, catsup and sherry. Work together until all lumps are gone and mixture is smooth and creamy.

Chicken and Celery Spread

2 cups ground cooked chicken
1 cup ground celery

½ cup mayonnaise
Salt to taste

Make a smooth mixture of ingredients. Spread on crackers or toasted rounds of bread. Garnish with sliced stuffed olives or pimientos if desired.

Chicken Balls

2½ cups cooked chicken, minced
½ teaspoon minced onion
¼ teaspoon salt

2 tablespoons mayonnaise
¼ cup sifted flour (about)
¼ cup melted butter (about)

Mix cooked chicken with minced onion, salt, and mayonnaise. Form into small balls. Roll balls in flour and dip in melted butter. Place in shallow biscuit pan. Heat in 400-degree oven until nicely browned. Serve hot.

Chicken Liver Paste

½ pound chicken livers
1 hard-cooked egg
1 medium-size onion

1 tablespoon butter
Salt, pepper, and tabasco to taste

Simmer livers in sufficient water to cover until barely done. Drain, and save water in which livers were cooked. Combine liver and hard-cooked egg. Mince onion, then sauté in butter. Add sautéd onion, butter drippings, and seasonings to livers and egg. Mash all with table fork. Then whip with fork until mixture is a paste. If too stiff for spreading, use small quantity of liver water for thinning.

Clam Dip

6 ounces cream cheese
1 pint cream-style cottage cheese
1 7-ounce can minced clams
1 teaspoon Worcestershire sauce

10 drops tabasco
½ small onion, finely grated
¼ teaspoon garlic powder
Dash salt

Drain clams and set liquid aside, while blending all other ingredients thoroughly. Pour clam juice a little at a time into above mixture until about the consistency of thick cream.

Cocktail Crackers

⅔ cup flour, sifted
½ teaspoon salt
6 tablespoons grated sharp
    Cheddar cheese

2 tablespoons butter
3 tablespoons milk
Dash of tabasco
6 ounces deviled ham

Sift flour with salt. Cut in grated cheese and butter. Add milk and tabasco. Mix well. Knead only until smooth. Spread with deviled ham. Roll up like jelly roll. Chill in refrigerator, preferably overnight. Slice the roll in thin slices. Bake on cooky sheet about 10 minutes in 400-degree oven.

Crab Meat Canape

7-ounce can crab meat
¼ cup finely minced celery
2 tablespoons minced pimiento

Mayonnaise
Rounds of toast

Flake the crab meat and mix well with celery and pimiento. Moisten with sufficient mayonnaise to hold mixture together. Spread on toast rounds.

Cucumber Finger Sandwiches

1 large cucumber (peel if desired)   1 tablespoon minced onion
Salt   Heavy cream
1 tablespoon lemon juice   Bread

Slice cucumber very thin. Sprinkle with salt and refrigerate for 30 minutes. Drain and rinse. Add lemon juice, onion, and sufficient cream to produce a mixture of spreading consistency. Spread between sandwich bread; cut into finger shapes.

Cucumber Slices

1 large cucumber   3 tablespoons sour cream
Salt   Tabasco
1 clove garlic, minced   Paprika
Dill (chopped sprigs if available)

At least one hour before serving time, peel cucumber and slice paper thin. Add garlic and dill. Sprinkle generously with salt. Let stand unrefrigerated for one hour or more. When ready to serve, drain water from cucumber and rinse. Combine with sour cream and tabasco. Sprinkle with paprika. Well liked at buffet meals.

Fresh Grapefruit Dip

4 ounces cream cheese   1½ teaspoons lemon juice
5 drops tabasco   ½ grapefruit
½ teaspoon Worcestershire   Paprika
   sauce   Chopped parsley

Mix cheese, seasonings, and lemon juice with blender or table fork until fluffy. Remove grapefruit sections; cut into small pieces. Add fruit and juice to cheese mixture. Spoon into grapefruit shell. These quantities provide about one cup of dip. Garnish with paprika and parsley. Place in center of hors d'oeuvres dish. Arrange apple wedges, cauliflower flowerets, cucumber fingers, carrot sticks around plate.

Guacamole

½ cup mayonnaise
½ cup commercial sour cream
2 tablespoons lemon juice
1 medium-size tomato, peeled and
finely chopped

½ cup minced onion, juice
pressed out
Salt, and white pepper to taste
Dash of tabasco
2 medium-size avocados, finely
chopped

Combine mayonnaise, sour cream, lemon juice, tomato, onion, salt, pepper, and tabasco. Add the avocado and mix gently. Chill well. These quantities should produce about 3 cups of dip for potato chips, corn chips, or tortillas.

Ham Pops

1 pound cooked ham, ground
(preferably Smithfield)
½ cup butter, melted
½ cup mayonnaise

⅔ cup peanut butter
1 clove garlic, minced
1 medium-size onion, minced
Dash of tabasco

Mix above ingredients well. Have ready the following biscuit dough:

4 cups flour
1 teaspoon salt
5 teaspoons baking powder

½ cup shortening
1 cup milk

Sift dry ingredients together. Cut in shortening and add sufficient milk to make a soft dough. Divide dough in half; roll one part very thin; spread thickly with ham mixture and cover with remaining dough also rolled thin. Press together lightly and cut in 1½ -inch squares. Bake on greased baking sheet in 425-degree oven about 10 minutes.

Liver Paste Canapés

2 pounds veal liver
2 medium onions
3 stalks celery
Juice of 1 lemon

Salt, pepper, and tabasco
2 hard-boiled eggs
Paprika
Bread rounds or round crackers

Simmer liver in water until tender. Remove skin and fibers. Grind in food chopper with onion and celery. Blend to a smooth paste, adding lemon juice, salt, pepper, and tabasco to taste. Spread on round crackers or bread rounds. Sprinkle with finely mashed eggs. Sift paprika on top.

Deviled Pecans

2 ounces butter
2 tablespoons soy sauce
Dash of tabasco

1 cup pecan halves
1 teaspoon salt

Melt butter in skillet over low heat. Stir in sauce and tabasco. Add pecan halves to butter mixture. Blend well. Add salt. Place pan in 400-degree oven for 20 minutes. Drain pecans and serve hot.

Potato Chip Mixture

2 hard-boiled eggs
1 tablespoon minced ripe olives
½ teaspoon salt
1 tablespoon finely chopped sour pickle

Pimiento (one whole)
Mayonnaise
Dash tabasco
Potato chips

Mash eggs with table fork. Add olives, salt, pickle, pimiento finely chopped, tabasco, and sufficient mayonnaise to hold ingredients together. Place by tablespoon on potato chips. Sufficient for 15 to 20.

Roll-ups

Roll piecrust very thin and cut into oblong pieces. Spread with desired filling and roll up like jelly roll. Chill rolls about 2 hours. Then cut into ½-inch slices and bake on greased cooky sheet in 425-degree oven about 15 minutes. *The following are suggested fillings:*

2 parts cream cheese to 1 part Roquefort.
Very sharp, grated Cheddar cheese, and finely chopped pimiento.

Sufficient mayonnaise to make it of spreading consistency.

Cream cheese, Roquefort cheese, and sherry.

Deviled ham and enough butter to make it of spreading consistency.

Sausage, cooked and mashed very fine, with crumbled bacon added.

Roquefort Cheese Canapé

½ pound Roquefort cheese	Dash tabasco
¼ pound butter	Paprika
1 teaspoon Worcestershire sauce	Toast rounds
3 tablespoons sherry	

Cream cheese and butter together. Add Worcestershire and tabasco, and sufficient sherry to make the mixture of good spreading consistency. Spread on toast rounds. Sprinkle with paprika.

Roquefort Dip

1 1½-ounce package Roquefort cheese (or blue cheese)	½ teaspoon Worcestershire sauce
1 3-ounce package cream cheese	Dash tabasco
Mayonnaise	Onion juice

Blend Roquefort or blue cheese with cream cheese. Add sufficient mayonnaise to make mixture of almost whipped-cream consistency. Add Worcestershire sauce and tabasco. A small amount of onion juice (about ¼ teaspoon) may be added if desired.

Seed Snacks

Piecrust dough	Caraway, poppy, or sesame seeds
Coffee cream (or 1 beaten egg mixed with 1 tablespoon water)	

Roll dough ¼ inch thick and cut into fancy shapes. Brush tops with cream or beaten egg mixed with water. Sprinkle with caraway, poppy, or sesame seeds and bake until brown in a 450-degree oven, about 10 minutes.

Shrimp Dip

1 cup sour cream
1 tablespoon prepared horseradish
½ teaspoon salt

¼ teaspoon paprika
Dash of tabasco
Shrimp

Add seasonings to sour cream, mixing thoroughly. Serve in small bowl on platter, surrounded by fresh shrimp.

Smoky Cheese Dip

1 glass smoky cheese spread
2 tablespoons coffee cream
1½ tablespoons mayonnaise
2 teaspoons fresh parsley, finely
   chopped

1 teaspoon onion juice
¼ teaspoon garlic powder
¼ teaspoon celery salt
½ teaspoon lemon juice

Blend all ingredients together thoroughly. Chill. Can be made ahead and stored in refrigerator.

Texas Toasts

Rounds of bread
Small white onions
¼ pound sharp Cheddar cheese,
   grated

1 teaspoon Worcestershire sauce
1 teaspoon dry mustard
Salt to taste
Dash of tabasco

Cut rounds of bread with small biscuit cutter and place a thin slice of onion on each. Cover with grated Cheddar cheese mixed to a paste with Worcestershire sauce, dry mustard, salt, and dash of tabasco. Heat under broiler until slightly brown. Serve piping hot.

Sandwiches

Avocado-Cucumber Sandwiches

Spread slice of bread with mayonnaise; place on it a layer of thinly sliced cucumber, followed by a layer of thinly sliced avocado. Sprinkle with salt and black pepper and top with another slice of bread spread with mayonnaise. Cut into triangles or use small cutters for fancier shapes.

Chicken Giblet Spread for Sandwiches

Grind 1 cup of cooked chicken giblets and mix with 1 tablespoon each of finely chopped pimiento, onion, green pepper; ¼ cup of finely chopped celery, ⅓ cup of finely chopped sour pickle, and ⅓ cup of mayonnaise. Season to taste with salt and black pepper.

Cream Cheese and Chili Sauce for Sandwiches

2 slices bacon, cooked crisp
1 3-ounce package cream
  cheese
1½ tablespoons chili sauce

1 tablespoon butter
Pinch of salt
Dash of tabasco

Crumble bacon finely. Soften cream cheese; add chili sauce, butter, bacon, salt, and tabasco, blending well.

Mushroom-Onion Sandwiches (open face)

Sauté in ¼ cup of butter, 2 tablespoons of finely chopped onion and 1 cup of thinly sliced fresh mushrooms. Cook for 5 minutes over very low heat; then add 4 hard-boiled eggs which have been mashed with a table fork, 2 tablespoons minced parsley, 1 teaspoon salt, ⅛ teaspoon black pepper, and dash of tabasco. Add 1 slightly beaten egg, blend well and cook until the mixture is thick. Spread on slices of bread, sprinkle with snappy Cheddar cheese and run under broiler until cheese melts. Cut into quarters or finger-size portions before serving.

Breads (Quick)

Batter Bread

2 eggs
1 cup white corn meal
1 teaspoon baking powder
2 teaspoons sugar

½ teaspoon salt
2 tablespoons butter, melted
1 cup boiling water
2 cups buttermilk

Beat eggs well and add dry ingredients (except baking powder) which have been sifted together, and then the melted butter. Pour on boiling water and stir vigorously. In 5 minutes (or when mixture is lukewarm) add buttermilk. Put small quantity of mixture into a cup and into it put baking powder. Mix well and return to batter. (I do this because otherwise it seems difficult to mix the baking powder thoroughly into the batter). Pour batter into well-greased pan, preferably iron (about 9″ in diameter and 3″ in depth), and bake about 30 minutes in 375-degree oven. In this particular recipe the boiling water does not seem to give the mush taste I object to in corn-meal breads, possibly because buttermilk has its own distinctive flavor. Neither do I object to sugar in this recipe although as a rule, like most Southerners, I do not care for it in corn bread.

Spoon Bread (*without leavening*)

According to old Southern cooks, for authentic spoon bread, the meal must be scalded and no other rising ingredient such as baking powder or soda added. The use of these rising aids make scalding of the meal unnecessary. In proof of this I offer the following recipe:

1 cup white corn meal	2 tablespoons butter, melted
½ teaspoon salt	1 pint milk
2 eggs (whites & yolks separated)	

Sift dry ingredients together. Add well-beaten egg yolks, melted butter, and milk. Fold in stiffly beaten egg whites. Pour batter into greased spider or casserole (about 8″ in diameter by 3″ in depth). Bake in 350-degree oven about 25 minutes.

I am also told that when soda and baking powder began to be used it was not necessary to make the batter for corn-meal bread as thin as the batter for true spoon bread and the name Batter Bread came into use.

Plantation Spoon Bread (*my favorite*)

4 cups milk	3 eggs
1 cup white corn meal	1 tablespoon butter, melted
1 teaspoon salt	2 teaspoons baking powder

Heat 2 cups milk to boiling point. Add meal (which has been sifted with the salt) slowly, stirring constantly, until thick. Remove from heat, cool to lukewarm, and add slowly to well-beaten eggs. Add butter and other 2 cups of milk. Sprinkle baking powder over top quickly and stir it in. Pour batter into greased casserole or spider (about 10″ in diameter by 3″ in depth) and bake 55 to 60 minutes in 350-degree oven until brown.

Corn Sticks or Muffins

1½ cups white corn meal (water-ground)
1 teaspoon salt
1½ cups boiling water

1 tablespoon melted butter
3 eggs
1½ cups milk

Sift corn meal and salt together. Pour boiling water over this mixture, stirring constantly. Cool to lukewarm. Add butter. Beat in eggs, one at a time. Stir in milk. Pour into hot, well-greased corn-stick pans. Bake in 425-degree oven 15 minutes or until well browned. Makes about 24 corn sticks, depending on size of pan. I usually use this recipe for corn-meal muffins rather than corn sticks.

Crackling Corn Bread

1½ cups white corn meal (water-ground)
½ teaspoon soda

½ teaspoon salt
1 cup cracklings
Buttermilk

Sift dry ingredients together. Mash cracklings and add to meal mixture. (Cracklings may be soaked in hot water in advance to make them more tender, and then drained.) Use sufficient buttermilk to make stiff batter. Form into small pones with the hand and bake in 350-degree oven about 30 minutes or until done. Makes about 8 pones. Traditionally in the South, corn pones have the imprint of three fingers on top.

Beaten Biscuits

4 cups flour
2 teaspoons salt

3 tablespoons lard or lard and butter mixed.
1 cup milk (about)

Sift flour and salt together. Cut shortening into flour mixture and slowly add sufficient milk to make a very stiff dough. Knead until smooth. Then beat with wooden mallet, on wooden meat block or other hard surface, until the dough blisters (about 45 minutes). Roll out to desired thickness. Cut out with small biscuit cutter. Prick top three times with a fork and bake in 450-degree oven until biscuits are a delicate brown.

Buttermilk Biscuits

2 cups flour
2 teaspoons baking powder
¼ teaspoon soda
   (Increase to ½ teaspoon if
   milk is very sour)

1 teaspoon salt
1 cup buttermilk (about)
2 tablespoons lard

Sift dry ingredients together and blend with lard. Add sufficient milk, about one cup, to make a soft dough. Roll out to ¼ to ½ inch in thickness; cut out with biscuit cutter. Place in biscuit pan or on baking sheet and bake in 350-degree oven about 10 minutes or until brown.

To make baking powder biscuits, use sweet milk, omit soda and increase baking powder to 3 teaspoonfuls. Step up heat to 375 degrees or 400 degrees and bake about 10 minutes or until desired shade of brown.

Animal fat makes a much softer biscuit than vegetable shortening and biscuits shortened with fat rendered from that old favorite of mine, country ham, are really out of this world. Similar fat from Smithfield hams is not suitable for this purpose, too much smoke or seasoning.

To render fat from ham which has been parboiled, cool the ham in the water in which it was cooked and skim grease from top. Put the grease in large frying pan on top of stove over low heat and cook until the water has cooked out. Keep heat low so that grease will not catch fire. Refrigerate after grease has cooled and use as shortening in bread.

Chicken Crackling Biscuits

3 tablespoons rendered chicken
   fat
¼ cup chicken cracklings
2 cups sifted flour

3 teaspoons baking powder
½ teaspoon salt
1 cup milk (about)

The yellow fat from a hen should be cut into small pieces and rendered over low heat until "cracklings" are golden crisp. Lift cracklings from liquid fat, cool, and refrigerate both until needed. Sift flour, measure and resift with baking powder and salt 3 times. Add cold chicken fat and cut in with a pastry blender or two knives. Add cracklings and stir only enough to distribute evenly. Add milk in 2 portions and mix in with a table fork. Do not stir. Dough should be soft but easy to handle. Knead very gently on lightly floured board and roll out to ½-inch thickness. Cut out with biscuit cutter and place on greased baking sheet. Bake 10 to 15 minutes in 450-degree oven or until biscuits are golden brown.

Orange Nut Bread

2 cups flour
1 teaspoon soda
1 teaspoon salt
½ cup sugar
1 egg
¾ cup strained orange juice

2 tablespoons lemon juice
1 teaspoon grated orange peel
¼ teaspoon grated lemon peel
¼ cup shortening
¾ cup pecan meats, finely
   chopped

Sift and measure flour; sift again with soda, salt, and sugar. Combine well-beaten egg, orange juice, lemon juice, grated peel, and shortening. Add dry ingredients and mix well. Add nut meats. Turn into well-greased pan (about 4 x 8″). Cover and allow to stand 20 minutes. Bake in 350-degree oven for about 45 minutes.

Corn-Meal Griddle Cakes *(The best, I think)*

1 egg (white & yolk separated)
1½ cups buttermilk
1 cup corn meal (or ½ cup
   each of flour and meal)
2 teaspoons baking powder
½ teaspoon soda

½ teaspoon salt
1 teaspoon light brown sugar
2 tablespoons butter, melted
   (other shortenings may be
   used)

Beat the egg yolk well and add the buttermilk and dry ingredients which have been sifted together. Add melted butter, then stiffly beaten egg white. Cook on hot griddle, well greased unless it is a soapstone griddle. Drop onto griddle from the end of mixing spoon in quantity desired. Turn only once, after bubbles appear on top side. If iron griddle is used, after first cakes are cooked, sprinkle griddle well with salt and cakes will not stick. This recipe makes about 12 cakes, 3″ in diameter.

Griddle Cakes *(using mostly wheat flour)*

Follow above directions, using 1 cup flour and 1 tablespoon white corn meal instead of all corn meal or flour and meal as indicated in previous recipe.

Blueberry Griddle Cakes

1 egg
1½ cups buttermilk
½ teaspoon soda
1 cup flour
1 tablespoon white corn meal
1 teaspoon baking powder
½ teaspoon salt

1 teaspoon sugar
2 tablespoons butter (or other
   shortening), melted
½ cup fresh blueberries or
   frozen berries, thawed and
   drained

Beat egg yolk and add buttermilk mixed with soda. Into this mixture sift flour, meal, baking powder, salt, and sugar. Pour in melted butter. Dust berries with a small quantity of flour and blend into batter. Then fold in stiffly beaten egg white. Fry on hot greased griddle. Makes about 12 cakes 3″ across.

Potato Pancakes

2 eggs, slightly beaten
1 cup milk
⅛ teaspoon fresh onion juice
Dash of tabasco
¼ cup flour

2 teaspoons baking powder
1 teaspoon salt
3 cups grated raw potatoes (4 large)

Combine eggs, milk, onion juice, and tabasco. Sift in dry ingredients and blend well. Fold in potatoes. Cook on hot greased griddle, turning when bubbles appear on top side. Cakes should be well browned on both sides.

Huckleberry Muffins

1 cup huckleberries
2 cups flour
3 teaspoons baking powder
½ teaspoon salt

½ cup shortening
1 cup milk
1 egg, well beaten

Wash and drain berries and sprinkle with ½ teaspoon flour. Sift dry ingredients and cut in shortening. To this add milk and beaten egg. Stir floured berries in quickly; don't mash them. Bake in hot greased muffin pans for 20 minutes in 350-degree oven. Makes from 12 to 15 muffins. Blueberries can be substituted.

Plain Muffins

2 cups flour
3 teaspoons baking powder
1 tablespoon sugar
½ teaspoon salt

2 eggs, well beaten
1 cup milk
4 tablespoons shortening

Sift together flour, baking powder, sugar, and salt; add eggs, milk, melted and cooled shortening, to make a stiff batter, stirring only until well blended. Half fill greased muffin tins and bake in 400-degree oven 18 to 20 minutes. Makes from 12 to 15 muffins. This makes a very rich, soft muffin.

Sour Cream Muffins

1⅓ cups flour	2 tablespoons sugar
1 teaspoon baking powder	1 egg
½ teaspoon soda	1 tablespoon soft butter
½ teaspoon salt	1 cup thick, sour cream

Sift dry ingredients together. To well-beaten egg, add butter and sour cream. Blend well. Add dry ingredients and stir only until moistened. Fill greased muffin pans half full. Bake in 400-degree oven 20 to 25 minutes. Makes 12 medium-size muffins.

Corn-Meal Mush

4 cups boiling water	1 teaspoon sugar
1 cup white corn meal	1 teaspoon salt
2 tablespoons flour	

To boiling water, in double boiler, add dry ingredients sifted together, stirring constantly until well mixed. Cook and keep stirring until mixture begins to thicken. Then cover and stir occasionally until mixture is very thick, which will require at least one hour. Serve hot with butter. If turned into loaf pan and left overnight it may be fried after being cut into inch slices. For this I prefer bacon grease. The mush browns more evenly if the heat is kept low.

Popovers (unbeaten)

2 eggs	1 cup flour
1 cup milk	½ teaspoon salt

Break eggs into bowl, add milk, and flour and salt sifted together. Mix well with spoon (ignore lumps). Fill greased muffin pans three-quarters full. Put in oven. Set control at 450 degrees. Turn on heat.

Bake about 30 minutes. Be sure to start baking with cold oven and no peeking for full 30 minutes. Makes 10 to 12.

Popovers

1 cup flour
¼ teaspoon salt
2 eggs

1 tablespoon melted shortening
1 cup milk

Sift together flour and salt. Make a well in flour, break eggs into well; add shortening and milk and stir until smooth. Fill greased muffin rings about half full and put into moderate (350-degree) oven for 20 minutes; increase heat to 450 degrees for 10 minutes; reduce heat to 350 degrees and allow to dry out for about 10 minutes. This reverses the usual routine as to baking, but I find I have greater success by using this method (not original with me) than by following the more orthodox procedure of putting popovers in hot oven, then reducing heat.

Hush Puppies

2 cups white corn meal
1 tablespoon flour
½ teaspoon soda
1 teaspoon salt

1 egg, beaten
3 tablespoons finely chopped onion
1 cup buttermilk

Mix dry ingredients; add beaten egg, onion, and buttermilk, and mix well. Melt enough shortening in frying kettle or deep skillet to make it 2½ inches deep. Drop batter by teaspoonfuls into hot (380-degree) fat, dipping the spoon first into hot fat, then into batter. Fry 6 or more hush puppies at a time. Cook until well browned on both sides. Drain on brown paper. 4 to 5 servings.

Buttermilk Waffles

1 cup flour
1 tablespoon white corn meal
1 teaspoon baking powder
½ teaspoon soda
1 teaspoon salt

1 teaspoon sugar
1 cup buttermilk
1 egg, separated
2 tablespoons melted butter or shortening

Sift dry ingredients together and add the buttermilk. Add well-beaten egg yolk, then melted and cooled butter or other shortening. Gently fold in stiffly beaten egg white.

Using more than one egg to this quantity of flour gives too "eggy" a product for my taste.

To use sweet milk, substitute an additional ½ teaspoon of baking powder for the soda.

Although I greatly prefer waffles baked on the stove in the old-fashioned irons (the kind that rest on an iron cuff, not flat on the stove), I think them pretty good made in an electric iron, using the above recipe. Even on a well-seasoned electric waffle iron, I like to spread a little cold shortening to prevent any sticking.

I use the above recipe on either kind of waffle iron, sometimes adding a little additional milk as I very definitely prefer waffles on the soft side.

Breads (Yeast)

Southern Split Biscuits

2 medium-size potatoes
½ cup melted butter
½ cup melted lard or other shortening
2 tablespoons sugar
1 teaspoon salt

1 cup milk
½ yeast cake
¼ cup lukewarm water
2 eggs, well beaten
6 cups flour
Melted butter

Peel and boil potatoes until thoroughly cooked. Mash fine with table fork or ricer. Add ½ cup melted butter, lard; then sugar and salt. Next add milk, and yeast which has been dissolved in lukewarm water. Add eggs and blend thoroughly. Add flour to potato mixture about 2 cups at a time, beating vigorously after each addition. Put dough in a well-greased covered bowl and set in warm place. Let rise until double in bulk; roll out to desired thickness. Cut with biscuit cutter. Place one on top of another after covering the bottom one with melted butter. Press together firmly. Allow to rise in warm place until light. Place on greased shallow biscuit pan or on baking sheet. Bake in 350-degree oven about 15 minutes or until golden brown.

Bread (*with eggs and potatoes*)

2 medium-size potatoes (retain water in which cooked)
½ cup melted shortening
¼ cup sugar
2 teaspoons salt
1 yeast cake

¼ cup lukewarm water
Milk, about ½ cup
2 eggs, unbeaten (with sufficient milk added to make 1 cup liquid)
6 cups sifted flour

Boil potatoes until well done, mash. Measure 1 cup of water in which potatoes were cooked. Combine potatoes and water. Add shortening, sugar and salt and mix well. Dissolve yeast in lukewarm water, then add to potato mixture, blending well. When mixture has cooled, add unbeaten eggs and milk, well blended.
Into another bowl sift flour; add liquid, a little at a time and blend into a soft dough. Knead on lightly floured board for 10 minutes. Place dough in bowl, cover and set in a warm place until contents doubles in bulk. Knead again on floured board. Shape into loaves and place in two well-greased loaf pans (9 x 5½ x 2½ "). Set in a warm place to rise. When doubled in bulk, bake in 400-degree oven for about 20 minutes. Then set oven back to 300 degrees and bake for about 20 minutes longer. Turn out on wire racks to cool.

Bread

1 cup milk
1 cup boiling water
2 tablespoons sugar
3 teaspoons salt

1 yeast cake
6 cups flour, sifted
2 tablespoons shortening

Scald milk. Add to boiling water and pour over sugar and salt. Stir until dissolved. Cool to lukewarm and crumble in the yeast. Add

3 cups of flour. Beat with a wooden spoon (preferably) until smooth and elastic. Beat in melted shortening. Add remaining flour about a cupful at a time, kneading until all the flour is used and the dough is smooth. Put in greased bowl and turn at once so that top side will be greased. Cover and let rise in a warm place for about one hour. Then punch down and let rise again until nearly double in bulk (about one hour). Divide dough in half, shape into two loaves and place in well-greased loaf pans (9 x 5½ x 2½"). Let rise until dough has reached top of pan (about an hour). Bake about 1 hour in 350-degree oven.

Rich Loaf Bread

4 cups sifted flour	3 tablespoons shortening (prefer-
¾ cup milk	ably butter)
2 tablespoons sugar	1 yeast cake
1 teaspoon salt	3 eggs

Sift flour before measuring. Scald milk; add sugar, salt, and shortening. Cool to lukewarm; add yeast and beaten eggs. Add half of the flour and beat 3 minutes. Add rest of flour, half a cup at a time and stir after each addition. Knead, shape, allow to rise until light, and bake.

Homemade Loaf Bread, Toasted

I used to think mere toast not a fitting bread to offer company at breakfast, but now I consider toast wonderful made by bread from any of the luscious recipes above. First toast on one side in the oven, then turn. Before toasting the other side, spread it generously with butter, then toast. Truly a delicious bread feast!

Salt Risen Bread

(I know it is usually called Salt Rising but to me the past tense seems preferable.)

4 cups milk
½ cup white water-ground corn meal
1 tablespoon salt

1 tablespoon sugar
5 tablespoons lard or other shortening
11 cups flour, sifted

Scald 1 cup of milk and pour over corn meal. Allow to stand until it ferments, about 24 hours. (I put the meal and milk mixture in a glass screw-top jar and keep it warm during the daytime by setting the jar in warm water. At bedtime I set the jar in a kettle on top of a baby-size hot-water bottle filled with boiling water. I then wrap a heavy towel or bath mat around the jar, put the cover on the kettle, and it keeps sufficiently warm until morning.) To make dough, heat until lukewarm 3 cups of milk to which the salt, sugar, and lard or other shortening have been added. Stir in 3½ cups of sifted flour. Then stir in the corn-meal mixture. Place bowl containing the flour-milk-meal mixture in a pan of lukewarm water for about 2 hours, or until bubbles work up from the bottom. Stir in 5 cups of flour. Knead in until smooth the remaining 2½ cups of flour. Then put in pans in which it is to be baked until doubled in bulk, which with me is usually about 4 hours in cold weather. I like to bake mine in 2 (9 x 5½ x 2½ ") small oblong black pans greased and the remainder in any sort of pan that is handy, sometimes an iron frying pan. Bake in 350-degree oven for about 15 minutes. Increase heat to 425 degrees and bake for about 45 minutes. This recipe makes lovely white bread.

Salt Risen Bread (*with egg*)

1 egg
1 cup white water-ground meal
Boiling water
1 quart milk

1 tablespoon salt
2 tablespoons sugar
10 (about) cups flour, sifted

Break egg into an 8-ounce measuring cup and stir in sufficient white water-ground corn meal (about 1 cup) to make a stiff dough. Pour boiling water into a cup and from cup onto egg and meal to fill cup two-thirds full, stirring until smooth. Do not pour boiling water directly on meal and egg as it would cook it. Put cup in warm place until morning. (See preceding Salt Risen Bread recipe for my method of keeping it warm during the night). Then scald 1 quart of milk (do not boil). Add to hot milk 1 tablespoon of salt and 2 tablespoons of sugar. Cool to lukewarm and add contents of cup which should have fermented well overnight (there should be bubbles). Then stir in 4 cups of flour. Put in gallon jar or container in warm place until it is bubbly. Add ½ cup lard, blending well. Then add sufficient flour to make moderately stiff dough. Set to rise in warm place and bake as directed in preceding recipe for Salt Risen Bread. Of all the recipes for my favorite bread which I have used in recent years, I believe I prefer this one.

Flannel Cakes

2½ cups flour, sifted
¾ teaspoon salt
2 eggs, separated

½ cake yeast
¼ cup lukewarm water
2 cups lukewarm milk

Sift together flour and salt. Add well-beaten egg yolks mixed with ½ cake of yeast which has been dissolved in lukewarm water and added to 2 cups of lukewarm milk. Beat until light. Fold in the well-beaten egg whites. Let batter rise covered, approximately 5 hours in a warm place. When light, bake on a hot griddle which has been greased lightly, turning only once preferably, when bubbles appear on surface. Cook until well browned on both sides.

Sally Lunn

Sally Lunn is one of Virginia's most famous breads. Probably only a few of her inhabitants today know that it takes its name from that of a baker's daughter in Bath, England. It is said she made a round loaf of bread which was best eaten while hot and that she used to hawk her wares through the streets of the old watering town in the middle 1700's. Her recipe seems to have arrived in Virginia at about the time relations with the Mother Country were severed. This is the recipe for Sally Lunn which I use most often. It takes four hours for the entire process.

¼ cake yeast
2 cups milk
2 eggs
2 tablespoons sugar

4 cups flour
1 teaspoon salt
2 tablespoons butter, melted

Dissolve yeast in ¼ cup of the milk which has been scalded and cooled to lukewarm. Beat eggs; add sugar and remaining milk to yeast mixture. Sift in flour and salt, and beat until perfectly smooth. Add melted butter (cooled) and beat again. Let rise until almost double in bulk. Beat down with a spoon, and then pour into well-buttered pan (preferably a Turk's head iron mold such as fruit cakes are baked in). Let rise to almost double in bulk. Bake in 350-degree oven for about 1 hour, covering after the first half hour.

Sally Lunn (with potato)

1 cup butter and vegetable
  shortening, mixed
5 cups flour, sifted
2 eggs
1 medium-size potato, thoroughly
  cooked

Potato water
2 tablespoons sugar
1½ teaspoons salt
½ yeast cake

Mix butter and shortening throughly into flour. Beat eggs well. Mash potato through a fine sieve into about 1 cupful water in which it was cooked. To this add sugar and salt and, when lukewarm, add ½ yeast cake. Let stand until yeast is dissolved; then mix with beaten eggs. Pour gradually into flour and knead until dough is soft and smooth. Put in well-greased bowl, cover and set in warm place. Let rise about 2 hours or until dough is twice its original size. Punch down and put to rise a second time in a large well-greased cake mold. This quantity makes 12 medium-size muffins in addition to one large loaf. Bake loaf for 1¼ hours in 350-degree oven. Serve hot. Pull apart with two silver table forks. Cook muffins in greased muffin rings 35 to 40 minutes.

Raised Muffins

¼ yeast cake, crumbled
1 tablespoon cooked potato,
   mashed and cooled
2 tablespoons shortening, melted
   and cooled
1 egg, well beaten

1 tablespoon sugar
3 cups flour, sifted
½ teaspoon salt
1 cup (about) milk, scalded and
   cooled

Add crumbled yeast, potato, and shortening to egg. Sift flour, sugar and salt together. Add flour and milk alternately to egg mixture until a fairly stiff dough is obtained. Beat to blend well. Place in greased bowl, cover and let rise about 2 hours in moderately warm place. One hour before serving time, fill well-greased muffin pans about ½ full. Let rise again and bake in 400-degree oven about 20 minutes.

100-per-cent Whole-Wheat Bread

½ cup brown sugar
⅔ cup lukewarm water
2 cakes yeast
1 tablespoon salt
2 cups milk, scalded

6½ cups unsifted whole-wheat
   flour
2 tablespoons shortening,
   melted

Stir 1 teaspoon of the sugar into water; add yeast and let stand 10 minutes. Mix remaining sugar and salt, and add to hot milk. Cool to lukewarm. Stir softened yeast, add milk mixture and blend. Stir in 3 cups of the flour; add shortening and mix well. Add remaining flour gradually and mix thoroughly. Turn onto lightly floured board (use 2 tablespoons of white flour for kneading and shaping loaves) and knead 10 minutes. Place in greased bowl; and turn at once to bring greased side up. Cover and allow to rise in warm place until doubled in bulk. Shape into loaf or loaves as desired. Place in well-greased pans. Grease top, cover and set in warm place until light enough for rounded tops to come above sides of pan. Bake in 400-degree oven for 10 minutes. Reduce heat to 375 degrees and bake

40 minutes longer or until done. Remove from pan to wire rack and cool uncovered.

Buckwheat Cakes

½ yeast cake
½ cup lukewarm water
1 pint lukewarm water

2 cups buckwheat flour (country ground)
1 cup sifted white flour
1 egg

Dissolve ½ yeast cake in ½ cup lukewarm water. Add this to 1 pint lukewarm water. Then add buckwheat flour and white flour, sifted. Make stiff batter. Beat in egg. Allow to rise about 8 hours in warm place. When ready to use, add:

1 tablespoon molasses
1 teaspoon baking powder

½ teaspoon soda
¾ teaspoon salt

Thin the batter with lukewarm water until of the desired consistency. Drop by spoonfuls onto greased griddle. Turn when bubbles appear on surface of cakes and cook until well browned.

Buttermilk Rolls

1 yeast cake
¼ cup lukewarm water
1 egg
3 tablespoons sugar

1 teaspoon salt
¼ pound butter, melted
1½ cups buttermilk
6 cups (about) sifted flour

Dissolve yeast in ¼ cup lukewarm water. Beat egg until light. Add sugar, salt, butter, and yeast. Beat well. Add milk and flour alternately until the dough is smooth and stiff. Knead well. Put in greased bowl in warm place and cover. Let rise until double in bulk (about 2 hours). Push down and allow to rise again. Roll out and cut with biscuit cutter. Place on greased baking sheet or in shallow biscuit pan, covered, in a warm place and let rise about 1 hour. Bake in 425-degree oven for about 20 minutes. Brush with butter when nearly brown.

Rolls

1 cup water
¼ cup shortening
1 yeast cake
⅔ cup lukewarm water

¼ cup sugar
1 tablespoon salt
1 egg
6 cups (about) sifted flour

Boil 1 cup water and let ¼ cup of shortening melt in it. Dissolve 1 yeast cake in ⅔ cup lukewarm water. When water and shortening mixture is lukewarm, add yeast with ¼ cup of sugar, 1 tablespoon salt, and 1 beaten egg. Mix well. Add gradually sufficient sifted flour (about 6 cups) to make a stiff sponge. Place in greased bowl; cover, and allow to rise until double in bulk (about 2 hours). Make into rolls, dip in melted butter, lay in buttered pan and allow to rise again, about 1 hour.
Bake in 400-degree oven.
I have also used this recipe for loaf bread, and for some reason it makes especially delicious toast.

Soups

Brunswick Soup

I dislike this made thick enough to be a stew, so I have paraphrased the name of this prime Virginia favorite. I seldom if ever feel that I can afford to put a whole chicken in it and consider anyway that the rich broth from a nice fat hen, well seasoned, is what gives it its delectable flavor; that and some sweet chutney.

1 quart of shelled lima beans

1 bunch celery, chopped (include a few leaves)

Chicken (leftovers or 3-lb. cooked fowl)

1 tablespoon apple or peach chutney

1 large onion, finely chopped

6 small tomatoes, chopped or large can tomatoes

Chicken broth (about 2 quarts)

Salt and pepper to taste

Small snip of hot red pepper

1 can corn (whole grain) or corn cut from 6 ears

Add lima beans, celery, chicken, chutney, onion, and tomatoes to broth, with salt, pepper, and piece of red pepper pod. Boil these together for about 30 minutes. Add corn and cook about 5 minutes longer. Check the seasoning as cooking progresses. (Several years ago when I was making peach chutney for the first time, I followed directions carefully, not realizing that the amount of ginger indicated was an exorbitant quantity to use, and twice as much as the one little tin I had contained. When I realized the mistake in the recipe I tried to rectify it, first by adding more vinegar to my chutney, which made it too tart, then more sugar. What finally evolved was almost a solid mass, not suitable for serving as chutney. One day when making Brunswick soup, I decided to try adding about a tablespoonful of my peach chutney. The result was the most deliciously flavored Brunswick soup I had ever tasted. Properly made chutney gives no such delicious results, but it does add to the flavor, especially if it is rather sweet. Sometimes in addition to chutney I add brown sugar to step up the flavor.) Serves 10–12.

Clam Chowder

¼ pound salt pork (streak o' lean-streak o' fat)
1 large onion, finely chopped
2 stalks celery, finely chopped
1 green pepper, finely chopped
3 medium-size potatoes

2 cups chopped fresh clams (canned chopped clams may be used)
Clam liquid
Salt and pepper to taste
Dash of tabasco
1 quart milk (or cream)

Remove rind from pork, dice and fry in large frying pan until well done. Add onion, celery, and green pepper. Cook until vegetables are soft. In the meantime, peel, dice and boil potatoes. Add clams and liquid (if necessary add sufficient water to make at least 1 cupful). Then add potatoes and at least 1 cupful of water in which they were cooked. Add seasonings and allow to simmer for 1 hour. When serving time comes, scald milk and add to the chowder, together with a small quantity of white sauce if desired. If cream is used, thickening will not be needed. Serves 10–12.

Mrs. George Washington's Crab Soup

(One hardly recognizes her by her correct social title, does one?)

8 hard-shelled crabs	1 quart sweet milk
2 hard-boiled eggs	½ cup cream
1 tablespoon butter	¼ cup sherry
1 tablespoon flour	Salt
Grated peel of 1 lemon	1 teaspoon Worcestershire sauce
Pepper	

Pick out the meat of the crabs which have been boiled half an hour. Set aside until needed. Mash hard-boiled eggs to a paste with a fork and add to them butter, flour, grated lemon peel, and a little pepper. Bring milk to boil. Pour gradually into well-mixed paste of eggs, etc. Put over low fire; add crab meat and simmer for 5 minutes. Add cream and bring to boiling point again. Then add sherry, salt to taste, and Worcestershire sauce. Heat sufficiently to serve, but do not boil after sherry has been added. Serves 10–12.

Cream of Chestnut Soup

1 pound Italian chestnuts	1 crushed allspice
½ cup finely chopped celery	Salt and pepper to taste
1 teaspoon finely chopped onion	Dash of tabasco
2 cups chicken stock	1 tablespoon flour
1 sprig thyme	2 tablespoons butter
1 crushed bay leaf	1 cup coffee cream
1 crushed clove	1 cup milk

Boil chestnuts until tender, about 20 minutes. Shell and mash to a fine paste. Place in saucepan and cover with water. Add vegetables, chicken stock, and seasonings. Boil until celery and onion are tender; thicken with flour and butter which have been rubbed to a paste. Then add cream and milk. Let boil up once and serve hot. Serves 6–8.

Curried Chicken Broth

6 cups chicken broth, strained
6 eggs
4 tablespoons lemon juice
½ teaspoon salt

¼ teaspoon black pepper
Dash of tabasco
3 tablespoons sherry
1 tablespoon curry powder

Bring chicken broth barely to boiling point, and gradually add beaten eggs to which lemon juice has been added, along with salt, pepper, and tabasco. Simmer for 30 minutes. Add sherry just before removing from fire. Then stir in curry powder. Refrigerate until very cold before serving.

Fruit Soup

2 cups orange juice
2 cups pineapple juice
Juice of half a lime

Sugar to taste
1 tablespoon plain gelatin

Combine juices and sugar. Add gelatin which has been dissolved in ¼ cup of lukewarm water. Refrigerate and after mixture begins to set, beat it with a fork. When ready to serve, beat well again with a fork.

Gumbo Filé

1 hen
1 large slice ham
1 tablespoon vegetable
  shortening
½ cup chicken fat
3 tablespoons flour
1 small onion
1 tomato, cut in small pieces
1½ quarts boiling water

1 bay leaf
3 sprigs thyme, or 1 teaspoon
  powdered thyme
Salt and pepper
Dash of tabasco
2 dozen oysters
3 sprigs parsley, chopped
2 tablespoons butter
1 tablespoon filé powder

Cut chicken up as for frying except in smaller pieces. Sprinkle with salt and pepper. Cut ham in small pieces. Put vegetable shortening and ½ cup of chicken fat into a frying pan; add ham and fry for about 15 minutes. Remove ham from fat and fry chicken on both sides until brown but not done. Remove chicken and add flour to make a thick sauce, stirring constantly until it is brown. Add onion, finely chopped, and cook until golden brown. Add tomato and cook for 5 minutes; add boiling water gradually, stirring well. Add ham, chicken, bay leaf, thyme, salt, and pepper to taste, and tabasco. Cook over moderate heat for 30 minutes or until chicken is tender. Add oysters, chopped parsley, and butter. Stir until well blended and cook for 5 minutes. Add filé powder slowly, stirring well. Serves 8–10.

Onion Soup

16 red onions
¼ cup olive oil
2 tablespoons sugar
Salt and pepper to taste

Dash of tabasco
8 cups beef stock
Bread rounds
Parmesan cheese

Peel onions and slice on bias. Simmer in olive oil until soft. Add sugar, salt, pepper, and tabasco. Put onions, juices and beef stock in casserole. Cut bread rounds from loaf of bread with a biscuit cutter, toast, cover each round generously with Parmesan cheese and float them on soup. Cover and put in 375-degree oven for 15 or 20 minutes. About 8 servings.

Orange Soup

3 tablespoons arrowroot
4 cups strained orange juice

1 cup sugar
1 tablespoon sherry or brandy

Rub arrowroot smooth in ¼ cup of water. Add to orange juice and cook until clear (about 20 minutes) over moderate heat. Remove from heat. Add 1 cup sugar and sherry or brandy. When sugar melts, chill soup. Serve in sherbet glasses with a little finely cracked ice and a garnish of finely chopped orange peel on top. Serves 6.

Peanut Soup

¼ pound butter
1 small onion, diced
2 stalks celery, diced
3 tablespoons flour
1 teaspoon salt
2 quarts chicken broth

1 pint peanut butter
⅓ teaspoon celery salt
Dash of tabasco
1 tablespoon lemon juice
Ground peanuts

Melt butter in saucepan and add onion and celery. Sauté for 5 minutes, but do not brown. Add flour, sifted with 1 teaspoon salt, and mix well. Add hot chicken broth and cook 30 minutes. Remove from heat, strain. While still hot, add peanut butter, celery salt, tabasco and lemon juice. Blend well. Just before serving sprinkle with ground peanuts. Serve immediately or reheat before serving. Serves 10–12.

Potato and Avocado Soup

6 tablespoonfuls butter
3 tablespoonfuls flour
1 onion, grated
2 teaspoonfuls salt
½ teaspoonful pepper

Dash of tabasco
6 cups milk
2 cups mashed potatoes
1 ounce white rum
1 avocado, cubed or sliced

Melt butter in saucepan; add flour and onion and cook, stirring until the mixture begins to brown. Season with salt, pepper, and tabasco. Scald milk in double boiler. Add flour-and-onion paste and mashed potatoes. Cook over boiling water, stirring constantly until mixture is the consistency of cream. Just before serving add rum and avocado. Serves 8–10.

Soup with Meat Balls

1 pound lean beef, finely chopped
2 eggs
Salt, pepper, and tabasco to taste
1 large onion
2 tablespoonfuls flour
3 garlic cloves

3 quarts chicken or beef stock
1 cup tomato juice (or 1 finely chopped tomato)
2 sprigs of fresh mint
2 sprigs of coriander

To finely chopped beef, add two well-beaten eggs and season with salt, pepper, and tabasco. Sift flour over meat mixture for easy handling and mold into small balls. Drop these into boiling soup stock which has been flavored with salt and pepper and tomato juice (or tomato). Serve hot. Add mint and coriander just before removing from heat. Serves 12–16.

Vichyssoise

2 bunches green onions
6 tablespoons butter
½ cup water
6 large potatoes
Few sprigs finely minced parsley
   and cress

2 cups strained chicken broth
1 cup coffee cream
Salt and pepper
Dash of tabasco

Chop onions fine and sauté for 5 minutes with butter in water. Dice potatoes fine and add with the onions, parsley, and cress to chicken broth. Simmer covered until soft (or about 15 minutes). Run through a sieve to make purée. Add cream. Season with salt, pepper, and tabasco to taste. Usually served completely chilled. Stir before serving. Serves 8–10.

White Soup

4 pounds veal knuckle
2 quarts cold water
3 carrots, sliced
1 onion, sliced
4 stalks celery
2 sprigs parsley
Bit of bay leaf

1 tablespoon salt
Dash of tabasco
¼ teaspoon white pepper
2 tablespoons sauterne
1 teaspoon beef extract
1 cup coffee cream

Cut meat from bone into small pieces. Put meat and bone in soup kettle, cover with water; add carrots, onion, celery, parsley, bay leaf, salt, tabasco, and pepper. Bring quickly to boiling point, reduce heat, simmer 5 hours, strain. Chill, remove fat, reheat; add wine, beef extract, and cream. Serves 12–16.

Meats

Stuffed Roast Beef (*oven cooked*)

4 or 5 pound roast
6 cloves garlic
Parsley
Celery tops
Green tops of onions
¼ lb. Parmesan cheese (in small chunks)

Suet
Salt and pepper
Dash of tabasco
Tarragon vinegar
Flour, sifted
Dry Burgundy wine
Hot water

Chop individually garlic, some parsley, celery tops, green tops of onions, Parmesan cheese, a little suet, salt and pepper, and dash of tabasco. Keep each ingredient separate. Rub roast lightly first with Tarragon vinegar. Take paring knife and cut holes in roast 2 inches apart. With fingers make holes deep enough to penetrate. Place a small amount of each ingredient in each hole. Put a small amount of flour on top. Add ¼ cup of dry Burgundy wine with every ½ cup of hot water (use about 1 cup of hot water when the roast is put in the oven). Bake covered until medium done. Take out and refrigerate for 24 hours. Put back in oven, basting with more wine and hot water and cook until done. Three to 4 servings to the pound.

Roast Beef

Set oven at 400 degrees. Sprinkle roast with salt and black pepper. If a slight onion flavor is desired, place 2 or 3 slices of onion on top of roast, or if preferred 2 or 3 small thin slivers of garlic may be inserted into deep cuts in roast. Put several small pieces of suet in roasting pan, no water. Put roast in pan and set in the oven. Allow to cook for about 20 minutes, or until slightly brown; then turn heat to 350 degrees and finish roasting. Time: 15 minutes a pound for rare roast, 18 minutes a pound for medium, or 20 minutes a pound for well done. This time schedule refers to a roast of 4 pounds or more. After roast is removed from pan, if more gravy is desired, add water. To my mind, flour is a destroyer of flavor in meat or poultry gravies. Three to 4 servings to the pound.

Hamburgers de Luxe

2 pounds ground sirloin	1 teaspoon black pepper
1 raw egg	2 tablespoons Worcestershire
2 cups chicken broth	sauce
½ teaspoon English mustard	2 teaspoons chicken fat
1 tablespoon salt	Dash of tabasco

Mix meat, egg and broth; then add other ingredients. Form into cakes and cook, in iron spider preferably, over moderate heat until done to taste. Serves 8.

Serve with braised onions or sauce, made as follows:

2 cups pan gravy from beef roast	1 tablespoon Worcestershire sauce
1 tablespoon English mustard	½ cup tomato catchup
2 teaspoons of any well-known brand of sauce for meat loaf, etc.	2 pats butter
	Parsley

Boil together 10 minutes, adding a little minced parsley. Pour over hamburgers.

Irish Beef Pasties

4 tablespoons butter
1 pound round steak, diced
¼ cup minced onions
1 cup diced raw carrots
1 cup diced raw potatoes
1 cup diced raw celery
1 teaspoon salt
¼ teaspoon black pepper

Dash of tabasco
1 tablespoon minced parsley
3 cups flour
4 teaspoons baking powder
¾ teaspoon salt
3 tablespoons shortening
1 cup milk

Melt butter in frying pan; add steak and brown. Add onion and cook for 2 minutes. Add vegetables, 1 teaspoon salt, the pepper, and tabasco; cover and cook gently for 10 minutes. Add parsley. Sift flour, baking powder and ¾ teaspoon salt together and cut in shortening. Add milk to make a moist dough. Roll out to about ¼ inch thickness and cut into 2 parts. Put half of the meat mixture on each piece of dough and fold over the edges to form a roll. Prick upper crust and place pasties on buttered baking sheet. Bake at 375 degrees for 25 to 30 minutes. Serve with Mushroom Sauce. Serves 8.

Mushroom Sauce
½ pound fresh mushrooms
¼ cup butter
¼ cup flour, sifted

1 cup milk (about)
¼ teaspoon salt

Wash mushrooms and cut in half if very large. Melt butter in top of a double boiler over low direct heat and add mushrooms. Cover, sauté until juicy, about 5 minutes. Blend in flour thoroughly. Add milk gradually (the amount to be added depends on the thickness desired). Cook over hot water until sauce is smooth and thick. Stir constantly; add salt.

High-Protein Meat Loaf

1 pound ground beef
1 pound ground pork
3 cups ready-to-eat high-protein
  cereal
½ cup finely chopped onions
¼ cup minced green pepper

3 eggs, slightly beaten
1 cup cooked tomatoes
3 teaspoons salt
½ teaspoon black pepper
Dash of tabasco

Mix all ingredients together, blending well. Press lightly in greased loaf pan. Bake at 350 degrees about 1½ hours. Let stand 5 minutes before turning out on hot platter. 8 servings.

Jellied Meat Loaf

1 tablespoon gelatin
½ cup cold water
2 cups hot meat stock
2 cups cooked meat, finely
  chopped
⅓ cup green pepper, finely
  chopped

⅓ cup celery, finely chopped
2 tablespoons onion, minced
Salt and pepper
Dash of tabasco
2 hard-boiled eggs

Pour cold water over gelatin and let stand for a few minutes; then add hot meat stock, the meat, green pepper, celery, minced onion; salt, pepper, and tabasco to taste. Turn into loaf pan, decorated with sliced egg. Chill until set. Unmold on a platter and slice. Serves 6–8.

Meat Loaf (by Martha)

1 pound round steak, ground
2 cups corn flakes or 1 cup fine
  bread crumbs
½ cup milk
1 teaspoon Worcestershire sauce

1½ tablespoons onion ground
  with steak (I always grind
  my own beef)
½ teaspoon salt
¼ teaspoon black pepper
Few drops of tabasco

Crush corn flakes slightly if used. Mix either corn flakes or bread crumbs well with other ingredients and pack in loaf pan, or form into loaf and put in iron frying pan or baking pan. Bake in 350-degree oven for 30 to 45 minutes. If better slicing consistency is desired, add 1 teaspoon of gelatin (dry) to ingredients and mix well. Serves 4 or 5. This mixture also makes good hamburgers.

Stuffed Meat Loaf

(loaf)

1½ pounds ground beef	1 egg, slightly beaten
½ pound ground pork	1 teaspoon salt
1 tablespoon minced onion	¼ teaspoon pepper
2 tablespoons horseradish	Dash of tabasco

Combine all ingredients, blend. Pat mixture into bottom and around sides of 9 x 5 x 3″ loaf pan to thickness of about 1 inch.

(stuffing)

4 cups mashed potatoes	2 tablespoons minced green
½ teaspoon salt	pepper
1 teaspoon paprika	2 egg yolks, well beaten
2 tablespoons minced pimiento	¼ cup milk

Combine ingredients in order given; blend well. Pack into meat-lined pan. Score top with tines of a table fork. Bake 1 hour (or longer to insure thorough cooking of pork.) in moderate (375-degree) oven. Serves 8.

Steak Butter

¼ of one clove of garlic, peeled	1 teaspoon lemon juice
¼ pound butter	½ teaspoon hickory salt
1 teaspoon minced chives or spring onions	Salt and pepper
1 teaspoon herbs (savory, basil, marjoram, etc.)	Dash of tabasco

Cut garlic. Rub bowl with it and then discard. Put butter in bowl and cream thoroughly. Blend in chives or onions, 1 teaspoon any preferred herb, lemon juice, hickory salt, black pepper and salt to taste, and tabasco. Blend well. When serving have Steak Butter at room temperature and spread on steak that is very hot.

Filet Mignon with Maître d'Hôtel Butter

Cut beef tenderloin in 1½ -inch slices; trim and press into circular shapes. Surround with thin slice of bacon, fasten with toothpicks and cook 10 minutes in a hot, well-greased frying pan, turning often. Remove to hot serving platter and spread generously with maître d'hôtel butter, made by mixing unsalted butter with chopped parsley, salt, pepper, tabasco, and lemon juice.

For flavoring steak, try putting a clove of garlic in olive oil, adding a few drops of tabasco and mixing thoroughly. Allow to stand for 5 minutes. Brush steak with mix before broiling, for flavor and brown crust.

Yorkshire Steak

2 pounds round steak, thick
Vegetable shortening
Salt and pepper
2 cups flour
2 teaspoons baking powder
1 teaspoon salt

2 egg yolks, beaten
1 cup milk
1 teaspoon Worcestershire sauce
Dash of tabasco
2 egg whites, stiffly beaten

Brown steak on both sides in shortening; season as desired with salt and pepper. Sift dry ingredients together and add egg yolks, milk, Worcestershire and tabasco. Mix well and fold in egg whites, stiffly beaten. Place steak in casserole or baking pan and pour over it the above mixture. Bake in 350-degree oven for about 1½ hours. Serves 6–8.

Swiss Steak

3 pounds round steak
Shortening
3 medium onions
1 pound fresh mushrooms
2 cloves garlic

1-#3 can of tomatoes
2 cups beef stock or
2 bouillon cubes
3 tablespoons flour, sifted
½ teaspoon pepper

Cut beef into ¾-inch slices. Dredge in flour seasoned with salt and pepper. Brown on both sides in a hot skillet, well greased. Place meat slices into a flat baking pan. Cover with sautéed onions, sautéed mushrooms, finely chopped garlic, strained tomatoes, and 2 cups beef stock or 2 bouillon cubes dissolved in 2 cups of hot water. Bake in a 350-degree oven 1½ to 2 hours. Serves 6–8.

Chile Con Carne

2 pounds dried red beans
3 pounds finely ground shoulder beef
¼ teaspoon cayenne pepper
4 tablespoons chili powder
½ teaspoon oregano
4 large onions
8 cloves of garlic

6 tablespoons olive oil
1 can tomato paste
2 large cans Italian type tomatoes
½ teaspoon marjoram
1 tablespoon monosodium glutimate
Salt to taste

Soak beans overnight. Boil for 1 hour (barely covered with water). In olive oil, sauté meat finely crumbled, with cayenne pepper, chili powder and oregano. Brown onions and pressed garlic cloves with the meat. Add this to the boiling beans. Add tomato paste, the tomatoes and marjoram. Add remaining seasonings and simmer for 5 hours. Serves 10–12.

Possibly because I grew up in Piedmont Virginia where a well-cured "country" ham is as highly prized as a Smithfield ham is down Richmond way, I still prefer them over all others and the recipes herewith were collected with them in mind, though in most cases Smithfield can be substituted. Both will usually be too salty unless soaked at least 12 hours in cool water.

When I lived in the country the designation in general use there was "old" ham. Now that I'm away from the country, I find that the term "country" ham seems to be a designation more easily understood by those from cities and towns.

Cooking Country Ham with Blanket (dough)

Use dough made in the proportion of 4 cups of flour to 1 cup of water. This dough is usually flavored with 1 cup of brown sugar to the above proportion of flour and water and 1 or 2 tablespoons each of the following spices: cinnamon, mustard, black pepper, cloves, and nutmeg to taste. If preferred, cider or vinegar may be used in place of water. Knead dough well after mixing thoroughly and roll out until there is sufficient to cover ham completely. The dough should be about ½ inch thick. It will not roll very readily. The ham should previously have been soaked for at least 12 hours and then well scrubbed (I use soap in the first water), to remove whatever curing ingredients were used and to clean the rind. Outside yellow fat should be trimmed off. With the ham completely covered with the dough, place in roasting pan, fat side up. Bake in 325-degree oven allowing 25 to 35 minutes to the pound. Remove dough blanket. Score top of ham diagonally, both ways, to form diamonds and top with favorite topping. Return ham to oven and bake until slightly browned. Some recipes call for breaking a hole in the crust during the last 30 minutes of baking and pouring in a cup of wine. A hammer or chisel would seem to be the best household tool available for breaking a hole in the crust.

Cooking Country Ham (with blanket made of yeast dough)

Soak ham at least 12 hours. In vessel large enough to let water cover ham, parboil until it is partially cooked (about 4 hours depending on size of ham). Remove from water, partly cool for handling purposes and remove skin. Then wrap in brown paper and over that place a blanket of yeast dough. Bake in 325-degree oven until done,

20 to 30 minutes for each pound of ham. Remove crust. Diamond score top of ham and cover with favorite topping. Return to oven until lightly browned.

Yeast Dough for Ham

1 cake yeast	1 teaspoon salt
1 cup scalded milk or boiling water	1 teaspoon black pepper
	1 teaspoon allspice
1 tablespoon brown sugar	4 cups flour

Dissolve yeast in ¼ cup lukewarm water. To 1 cup scalded milk or boiling water add sugar, salt, black pepper, and allspice. Add flour gradually, making a dough soft enough so that it can be easily stretched to cover the ham. Add softened yeast and beat to blend well. In doing some final rechecking and revising, in one of my older cookbooks (*Mrs. Hill's New Cook Book,* copyrighted 1870) I found a newspaper clipping which I think will be an interesting addition to the recipes for cooking a Smithfield ham.

HOW TO COOK A HAM

Smithfield, June 2, 1891.

To the Editor of the Dispatch:

The best mode of cooking a bacon ham seems to have aroused some attention through your columns. The following directions were followed by a citizen of this town more than 120 years ago, and have been continued in the families of his lineal descendants to the present (the fourth) generation:

Put a Smithfield ham of eight pounds into a kettle of cold water before it is placed on the stove or over the fire, and let it remain therein for three hours from the time the water begins to boil. For each additional pound in the weight of the ham the boiling must be prolonged thirty minutes.

This method is practiced by most of our citizens and is deemed the best, as well from a gustatory as a sanitary standpoint.

OCTOGENARIAN

Ham Cooked in Coca-Cola or Ginger Ale

Put a 12-pound ham, preferably "country," in a deep vessel and pour in sufficient Coca-Cola or ginger ale to half cover ham. Set on low heat, cover and boil until ham is tender. Test by sticking long tines of kitchen fork in ham. As liquid boils out, add more coca-cola or ginger ale. When done, take ham out and remove skin. As ham will have a somewhat sweet flavor the use of only bread crumbs as topping is suggested. Brown in 325-degree oven.

Country Ham, cooked with "Spirits"

Ham should be parboiled in a container sufficiently large for the ham to be completely covered with water while it is cooking. In this way, it can be cooked uniformly without turning the ham over, a somewhat hazardous business, believe me. Wash boilers of copper or galvanized tin, or large canners can be pressed into service as a container. Put the ham in, flesh side down, cover completely with cold water and when it begins to boil, turn heat down and cook slowly, allowing 20 minutes a pound. Add to water, 1 cup of white wine or gin, and a handful of hay (dried clover, supposed to draw impurities out). When ham is done, leave it in the water until it is completely cool. Then remove from vessel in which it was cooked and allow to drain for several hours on a platter or in a shallow pan. Remove skin and trim off any yellow fat or rough edges. Score top of ham in diamonds or squares; cover with mixture of equal parts of brown sugar and fine bread crumbs. Brown in 325-degree oven. Baste with juice of spiced or brandied peaches.

Fried Country Ham with Red Gravy

I believe Kentuckians call it "Red-Eye" gravy, as do some Virginians. At home we simply said red gravy.

Slice through the middle of the ham to the bone for serving size slices. Slice about ¼ inch thick, leaving fat attached. Cook ham over low heat in heavy frying pan until browned on both sides. A light sprinkle of sugar on each side before cooking intensifies the flavor. Pour off the grease when ham is removed from pan. Then put about ¼ cup of cold water in the pan and allow to boil up. Pour this over ham and grease which have been placed on a platter. To make "redder" gravy, before putting water in pan in which ham was cooked, add 1 tablespoonful of brewed coffee or ½ teaspoonful of sugar.

Baked Ham Slice

This recipe refers to what, when I was growing up, we called "Western" ham, on which I turned a very cold shoulder until recent years. There has been a very great improvement in the curing of this type of ham, hence the inclusion of a recipe applicable to such hams.
Ham slice 1½ to 2 inches thick. Slash fat edges at 1-inch intervals and dot with whole cloves. Bake ham in open pan in a 325-degree oven, allowing 30 minutes a pound for entirely uncooked ham. Baste several times while baking with pineapple juice. Garnish platter on which ham is served with pineapple slices and frosted grapes. To frost grapes, wash and drain them; dip in slightly beaten egg whites, roll in sugar, and set to dry.

Ham Cooked in Wine

Soak ham 12 hours in cold water. Remove from water and parboil in ½ gallon of sauterne for 4 hours (about), depending on size of ham. Let stand 12 hours again in sauterne and reheat the next day for easy peeling. Top with favorite topping; then bake uncovered until brown with about 2 cups of sherry, basting frequently.

To Cook a Ham (*very old recipe*)

Cover an 8-to-9-pound "country" ham with cold water and let soak 12 hours. Remove from water. Scrub with a stiff brush. Cover with fresh cold water and simmer 3 hours. Cool ham overnight in stock. Drain and remove skin. Place ham in uncovered baking pan or roaster. Cover with paste made of 4 cups of brown sugar and 1 cup of apple or peach brandy. Bake in 300-degree oven for 1½ to 2 hours. Remove and diamond score fat side. Stick cloves or whole allspice all over the top and sides. Return to oven and brown, basting frequently with drippings.

Ham (a Packer's Ham Ready to Cook)

Make thick paste of 1 cup of brown sugar, 1 cup strained honey, and 1 tablespoon of dry mustard. It must be thick enough to stick well. Coat ham with paste and dot it with whole cloves. Then mix 4 pounds of flour and sufficient beef bouillon to make a stiff dough. Add and blend well ½ cup of chopped herbs, consisting of parsley, chives, tarragon, spring onions, garlic, sage, and nutmeg, and 1 teaspoonful of caraway seeds. Wrap ham tightly in dough blanket, overlapping edges well and pressing together so that juices will not run out. Brush dough with brandy or juice from sweet pickles. Cut round hole in top of dough blanket and make stopper for it of dough, rolled in flour. Bake ham in 325-degree oven until dough is set hard. Remove ham from oven, take out stopper, and pour in as much brandy as sugar-honey topping will absorb. Replace stopper and continue baking about 1 hour longer, or until crust is thoroughly cooked and browned. Remove crust before serving.

Additional Ham Toppings

Mix 5 tablespoons brown sugar with 1 tablespoon flour and ¼ teaspoon ground cloves. Add sufficient water to make a paste. Cover top of ham with this after skin has been removed and bake in 375-degree oven for 1½ hours. If desired, 15 minutes before cooking is completed, baste ham with sherry or port.

Coat scored (cooked) ham with peach preserves half an hour before taking it from oven.

Cover ham with well-beaten egg, then rub in fine bread crumbs and brown in oven.

Use 1 cup of honey or molasses and spread over ham. Dot with cloves. Brown in oven.

Boil juice from 1 small can of sliced pineapple with ½ cup of brown sugar and 1 tablespoon of dry mustard until syrupy. Spread on ham and brown.

Cover fat side of ham with whole cloves. Mix 1 cup of vinegar and 1 cup of brown sugar. Put ham in open pan and pour vinegar-sugar mixture over it. Place in 325-degree oven to finish baking (having been previously parboiled).

Baste ham frequently with the liquid that has run off into pan. Bake ham until well browned.

Chill ham thoroughly before slicing if thin slices are desired (which is better if the carver will give you two).

Applesauce Apples (as garnish for whole cooked ham)

1 envelope gelatin
¼ cup cold water
1 can (20 ounces) applesauce

½ cup sugar
¼ teaspoon nutmeg
3 tablespoons lemon juice

Sprinkle gelatin on cold water to soften. Place over boiling water and stir until gelatin is dissolved. Add to applesauce with sugar, nutmeg, and lemon juice; blend well. If desired, applesauce mixture may be tinted red with vegetable coloring. Turn mixture into 5 custard cups; chill until firm. Unmold and place around cooked ham. Insert mint in molded jelly turned up to resemble apple leaves. Makes 5 servings.

Hog Jowl (Cured) and Turnip Greens

Wash jowl until clean, then put into boiling water to cover. Cook 45 minutes or until jowl is almost done. Add panful of well-washed and drained young turnip greens. Cook gently for another hour or more. Serve jowl in center of a platter with greens around it. Garnish with poached eggs. Serve potlikker in separate dish to be used for dunking corn bread.

Baked Ham Loaf

½ pound ground smoked ham
½ pound ground beef
½ pound ground pork
½ cup bread crumbs
1 egg

1 6-ounce can tomato purée or juice
Tomato sauce or grilled pineapple slices

Combine ham, beef, pork, bread crumbs, egg, and tomato purée. Put in a loaf pan. Steam for 1 hour. Then bake in 350-degree oven for ½ hour. Serve with tomato sauce or grilled pineapple slices. Makes 8 portions.

Individual Ham Loaves

1 pound ground ham
1 pound ground pork
½ cup cracker crumbs
3 tablespoons chopped onion
½ teaspoon salt
⅛ teaspoon black pepper

Dash of tabasco
2 eggs
½ cup milk
½ cup brown sugar
1 teaspoon dry mustard
2 tablespoons vinegar

Combine ham, pork, cracker crumbs, onion, salt, pepper, and dash of tabasco. Beat eggs, add milk and blend with first mixture. Form 8 balls and place in large muffin pans. Shape balls so meat is higher in center and does not come to top around edges. Bake in 350-degree oven for 20 minutes. Combine brown sugar, mustard and vinegar, blending until smooth. Boil 1 minute. Pour this syrup over meat loaves; bake about 40 minutes longer.

Pork Chops Baked in Sour Cream

4 loin pork chops, ½ inch thick
½ cup water
1 bay leaf

2 tablespoons vinegar
1 tablespoon sugar
½ cup sour cream

Wipe chops with damp cloth. Season with salt and pepper; dredge with flour and brown in a small amount of fat. Insert 1 clove in each chop and place in casserole. Add other ingredients, cover and bake in 350-degree oven about 1½ hours or until chops are done. Serves 4.

Salt Pork de Luxe

Slice salt pork (streak o'lean-streak o' fat kind) medium thin. Soak 1 hour in 1 cup of water and 1 tablespoon of molasses. Drain, then dip in flour and fry in ½ inch of fat until crisp and golden brown. Serve with cream gravy.

Fried Apples

Cut off slice at stem and blossom end and peel once around the middle of firm tart apples. Make thin slices up and down the apples to the core. Wash slices. Use sufficient hot-bacon or streak-o'-lean-streak-o'-fat-salt-pork grease to cover well bottom of frying pan. Put apples in frying pan with about 1 cup of light brown sugar and cook uncovered until practically done. Add ¼ cup of water and cover pan so that apples can steam until thoroughly done. Serve with bacon or salt pork. Food for the gods!

Pork Chops in Vermouth

4 loin chops, cut 1½ inches thick
Salt
Sage
½ cup stock or consommé
1 clove garlic
½ cup dry French vermouth
1 cup sour cream
Dash of tabasco

Brown chops well in heavy frying pan. Dust upper sides with salt and a little sage. Add stock and garlic. Cover and simmer on top of stove until tender, or about 1 hour. Add Vermouth, sour cream, and tabasco to chops and juices in pan, blending well. Let boil up, turning chops during the process. Serves 4.

Savory Pork Chops

6 pork chops, 1½ inches thick	Brown sugar
Salt	1 cup tomato catsup
Pepper	1 cup water
Lemon slices	

Place pork chops in a baking pan and sprinkle with salt and pepper. Place ¼-inch thick slices of lemon on each chop; sprinkle 1 teaspoon of brown sugar over each. Mix together 1 cup tomato catsup and 1 cup water and pour around chops until they are just covered. Bake in 350-degree oven for about 1 hour or until tender and well done. Serves 6.

Roast Lamb

Place 6-or-7-pound leg of lamb in open roasting pan. Make about six little cuts in it with a small pointed knife. Into each put a tiny sliver of garlic. Cover each cut with a small piece of fat cut from the lamb. Sprinkle with salt and black pepper and put in the oven, no water and no fat added. Turn gas as low as possible. (In my gas stove this would be about 250 degrees.) Roast for 4 or 5 hours. If electric stove is used, set heat regulator at 150 degrees and roast for 7 to 8 hours. This slow cooking gives a delicious leg of lamb.

Bewitched Liver

This recipe is from what in Lynchburg used to be considered a sort of cook's Bible, *Housekeeping in Old Virginia* by Mrs. Marion Cabell Tyree, copyrighted in 1879, published for some reason, in Louisville, Kentucky. I have recently been able to buy a copy, evidently a reprint, at a very reasonable price. Before that I had to borrow pages of it from a friend who is the fond possessor of a first edition, now falling apart from frequent use.

3 pounds veal liver, chopped fine. [I have fallen into using the Northern term "calves'" liver which my butcher tells me came South via the chain stores and is incorrect as calves are not marketed until they have reached the veal stage.]

1 cup grated bread crumbs
2 eggs, well beaten
¼ pound salt pork, finely chopped
2 teaspoons salt
2 teaspoons black pepper
½ teaspoon red pepper

Mix all well together, and put into a tin mould; set it in a pot of cold water and let it boil 2 hours. Then set the mould in a cool oven to dry off a little; when thoroughly cold turn it out—Mrs. J. H. (Most of the recipes in this old book were contributed by Mrs. Tyree's friends and were signed either with their full names or initials.)

Sausage Loaf

1 pound pure pork sausage
1½ pounds ground round steak
2 medium-size onions, chopped fine
1 cup finely chopped green pepper
1 cup diced celery
1 cup bread crumbs
Salt and pepper
Dash of tabasco
1 small can tomato sauce

Mix sausage and ground round steak well. Add onions, green pepper, and celery. Then add bread crumbs, salt, pepper, and tabasco. Blend thoroughly with meat mixture. Form into a loaf. Place in baking dish and pour tomato sauce over it. Bake in moderate oven (350 degrees) about 1 hour. Serves 6–8.

Barbecued Spare Ribs

3 pounds spareribs
⅓ cup water
⅓ cup butter
3 tablespoons prepared horse-radish
Dash of tabasco
3 tablespoons Worcestershire sauce
¾ cup vinegar
⅓ cup chili sauce
½ teaspoon salt
⅛ teaspoon black pepper

Lay spareribs on broiler rack or place in large pan and broil 30 minutes or until brown and crisp, basting occasionally with sauce made from all the other ingredients mixed together.

Liver Loaf

1 pound beef liver
1 cup boiling water
2 small onions
½ pound pork sausage
1 cup finely crushed corn flakes
1 teaspoon Worcestershire sauce
1 tablespoon lemon juice

1 teaspoon salt
½ teaspoon celery salt
⅛ teaspoon black pepper
Dash of tabasco
2 eggs, well beaten
1 slice bacon

Simmer liver in boiling water for 5 minutes. Drain, saving the liquid. Grind liver and onions in food chopper. Add sausage, corn flakes, seasonings and eggs. Add sufficient liquid to moisten slightly. Blend well. Pack mixture into a greased 8 x 4 x 3″ loaf pan, or shape and put in iron frying pan. Place bacon strip on top. Bake in 350-degree oven about 45 minutes or until done. Serves 8.

French Fried Liver Steaks

1 pound beef liver (sliced in
  ½ -inch slices)
½ cup fine dry bread crumbs or
  cracker crumbs
1 egg

2 tablespoons water
1 teaspoon onion juice
½ teaspoon salt
⅛ teaspoon white pepper
Dash of tabasco

Add water and seasonings to egg and beat well with a fork. Remove outside membrane from liver slices (usually on outside edges of slices only). Dip slices in crumbs, then in egg mixture and again in crumbs. Put 2 slices of liver at a time in frying basket. Lower into deep fat which has been heated to 350 degrees. Fry 3 to 4 minutes or until a golden brown. Serves 3–4.

Oxtails in Wine

2 oxtails, cut in 2-inch lengths
¼ cup flour
3 tablespoons shortening
½ cup chopped onions
½ cup chopped celery tops
¼ cup liquid in which oxtails
were boiled

½ cup red wine
1 teaspoon salt
⅛ teaspoon black pepper
Dash of tabasco
1 bay leaf
¼ teaspoon thyme
2 teaspoons flour

Parboil oxtails until tender, usually about 1 hour. Brown onions and celery tops in shortening. Add stock, wine, and seasonings. Dredge oxtails in ¼ cup of flour and put with the mixture in baking pan and cook until brown. Thicken gravy with 2 tablespoons of flour if desired. 4 portions.

Veal Casserole

1 large veal cutlet or 4 loin veal
chops
Shortening
2 medium-size onions
1 cup green peas
1 bay leaf
2 tablespoons flour
1 teaspoon marjoram

½ teaspoon thyme
2 tablespoons shortening
½ cup coffee cream
1 teaspoon Worcestershire sauce
Salt and pepper
Dash of tabasco
¼ cup sherry

Cut veal in serving pieces and brown well in shortening in heavy frying pan. When nearly done, add onions thinly sliced, and cook partly. Remove veal to buttered casserole, placing peas and onions on top of it. Add bay leaf. Put flour, marjoram, and thyme in frying pan with 2 tablespoons shortening and smooth to a paste. Add cream, Worcestershire sauce; salt, pepper, and tabasco to taste. Pour over veal and vegetables. Add sherry. Cook in 350-degree oven for 45 minutes. Serves 4.

Veal Paprika

4 slices breakfast bacon
1 pound veal, sliced thin
1 teaspoon onion, chopped fine
1 cup sour cream

1 cup tomato sauce
¼ teaspoon salt
⅛ teaspoon black pepper
1 teaspoon paprika

Cook bacon in frying pan. Brown veal in bacon fat. Brown onions; add sour cream, tomato sauce, salt, pepper, and paprika. Cover and simmer about 20 minutes. Bacon strips may be placed on top of and served with veal. Serves 3–4.

Veal Cutlet, Provençal

Flour a veal cutlet and fry in olive oil until brown. Add ¼ pound of fresh mushrooms cut in small pieces and let all simmer for 5 minutes. Sprinkle with 1 clove of garlic, peeled and finely minced. Pour in 2 ounces of dry white wine. Peel and finely chop 2 fresh tomatoes. Add to the veal-mushroom mixture, seasoning to taste with salt, black pepper, and a dash of tabasco. Cover and allow to simmer for 15 minutes. When ready to be served, sprinkle with minced parsley. Serves 3 or 4 depending on size of cutlet.

Swiss Veal

1½ pounds tender veal cut in thin
  strips about ½ inch wide
1 medium onion, finely chopped
2 large mushrooms, thinly sliced
6 tablespoons butter
1 cup light cream

1 tablespoon flour, sifted
Salt and pepper
Dash of tabasco
1 cup dry white wine
1 tablespoon parsley, finely
  chopped

Heat a heavy frying pan over moderate heat. Add butter. When butter has melted mix veal, onion, and mushrooms and sauté in the butter, stirring frequently until they are slightly browned, or for about 10 minutes. Blend cream with flour, salt, pepper and tabasco to taste, and add to veal mixture. Cook, stirring until mixture boils.

Turn heat low, cover and simmer until veal is tender, from 5 to 10 minutes. Mix wine and parsley. Add to veal mixture and allow to come to a boil once, stirring constantly. Turn heat to very low, cover and let simmer about three minutes. Serve at once. 6 servings.

POULTRY

Barbecued Chicken

Use 2 young chickens or 1 roasting size chicken, cut up as for frying. Wash and dry. Roll in flour. Brown chicken pieces in hot shortening. Season with salt and pepper. Take pieces of chicken from fat and place in open roasting pan. Bake for about 1½ hours in 350-degree oven. Baste frequently with the following barbecue sauce:

Melt ½ cup butter in saucepan. Add ½ cup vinegar, 1 tablespoon dry mustard, 1 tablespoon prepared mustard, 2 tablespoons grated onion, ¼ cup Worcestershire sauce, ½ cup tomato catsup, 2 tablespoons lemon juice, 1 clove garlic, finely minced, ½ teaspoon salt, 1½ teaspoons sugar, ¼ teaspoon tabasco. Simmer about 15 minutes to blend seasonings.

Broiled Chicken

Chicken should not weigh more than 2½ pounds, dressed. Split in half; wash thoroughly and wipe as dry as possible. Cut through wing and leg joints. Rub surface of chicken with a cut lemon, squeezing out some of the juice to insure sufficient liquid. Sprinkle with a mixture of approximately 2 teaspoons of salt, ¼ teaspoon black pepper, and ½ teaspoon paprika, depending on size of chicken. Coat well with melted butter and sprinkle lightly but completely with sugar. Put chicken in broiler pan (do not use rack) skin side down and flatten as much as possible. Place in broiler as far from heat as possible for approximately 10 minutes, to allow seasonings to penetrate slightly. Then raise to something like 4 inches from heat.

Broil slowly, turning as each side browns and basting with each turning. Should cook in about 35 minutes.

Chicken Country Captain

1 2-pound frying chicken
1 cup flour
½ cup butter
1 onion, finely chopped
Pinch of sage
1 green pepper, finely chopped
2 fresh tomatoes, chopped, or 1
   cup canned

½ cup unsalted pecans
½ cup seedless raisins or currants
1 cup water
Salt and pepper to taste
Dash of tabasco
4 ounces peach brandy (optional)
2 cups hot buttered rice

Disjoint chicken and cut into 8 pieces. Roll in flour and fry lightly (about 15 minutes) in butter over moderate heat until browned. Remove chicken from pan; add onion, sage, green pepper, tomatoes, pecans, raisins and 1 cup water. Bring mixture to a boil, then replace chicken in pan. Cover and simmer for 50 minutes. About 5 minutes before chicken is done season and add brandy if desired. Serve over rice. Serves 4 to 5.

Chicken Croquettes

3 tablespoons butter
4 tablespoons flour
1 cup hot chicken stock
½ cup heavy cream
3 cups finely chopped cooked
   chicken (turkey may be substituted)
1 tablespoon shallots (or spring
   onions)
¼ cup grated cocoanut (optional)

1 teaspoon lemon juice
1 tablespoon minced parsley
Salt, pepper, and tabasco
3 egg yolks
Flour
1 egg
¼ cup milk
1 tablespoon salad oil
Bread crumbs

Melt butter in saucepan and stir in flour, adding the chicken stock gradually. Cook sauce over low heat until thick and smooth. Add cream and chicken. Then shallots, cocoanut, lemon juice, parsley, salt and pepper to taste, and tabasco (just a dash). Blend well. Remove from fire and cool slightly. Stir in egg yolks, beaten slightly. Refrigerate until cold. Then mold into desired shape and roll in flour. Beat together 1 egg, ¼ cup of milk, and oil. Brush croquettes with the mixture. Roll in bread crumbs and fry in deep fat, if feasible (350 to 365 degrees), until browned, or fry in fat in frying pan, over moderate heat, turning frequently until brown all over.

Fried Chicken

Personally, I prefer fried chicken simply coated with flour, since it's the chicken I like rather than the batter in which it may be fried as follows: Cover cut-up fryer for at least 1 hour with sweet milk. Mix 1 egg, beaten slightly, ½ cup sweet milk, salt and pepper to taste, and dash of tabasco. Drain chicken and dip in this mixture; roll in flour. Fry in deep fat (350 degrees) about 20 minutes, or about half covered with vegetable shortening in a heavy frying pan, over moderate heat about 30 minutes, turning until it is a golden brown on all sides. Reduce to low heat, cover, and continue to cook very slowly until done, turning occasionally to brown evenly.

Oven-Fried Chicken

1 frying chicken cut up in serving pieces
½ cup melted fat or salad oil
Dash of tabasco (blend well into shortening)

¼ cup flour
¼ cup fine dry bread crumbs
1 teaspoon salt
¼ teaspoon black pepper

Wash and dry chicken thoroughly. Pour fat or oil into a baking pan. Set oven for 400 degrees. Combine flour, bread crumbs, salt, and pepper. Dip chicken in flour mixture to coat, and place it in the pan. Bake about 1 hour, turning as necessary to brown chicken on all sides.

Jellied Chicken, à la King

1 envelope plain gelatin
¼ cup cold water
2 eggs
½ teaspoon salt
¼ teaspoon paprika
Few drops tabasco
1¼ cups hot chicken stock
1 tablespoon lemon juice

½ cup coffee cream
1½ cups diced cooked chicken
2 tablespoons chopped pimiento
2 tablespoons chopped green pepper
2 2-ounce cans sliced mushrooms

Soften gelatin in cold water, or in ¼ cup liquid from mushrooms. Beat eggs; add salt, paprika, tabasco, and chicken stock, and cook in double boiler until consistency of thick gravy, stirring frequently. Add softened gelatin and lemon juice and stir until gelatin is dissolved. Add cream. Refrigerate and when mixture begins to thicken, fold in the chicken, pimiento, green pepper, and mushrooms. Pour into mold which has been rinsed in cold water and chill until firm. Unmold on platter, garnish with greens, and serve with mayonnaise.

Chicken Pudding

Some recipes for this favorite Virginia dish call for removing wings and legs and baking those with the rest of the chicken left whole in the batter. The following is my favorite version:

1 3-or 4-pound fryer, cut up
½ cup flour
1 teaspoon salt
¼ teaspoon black pepper
3 tablespoons vegetable shortening
1½ cups flour

1 teaspoon salt
1½ teaspoons baking powder
4 eggs, well beaten
1½ cups milk
Dash of tabasco
3 tablespoons butter, melted

Mix ½ cup flour, 1 teaspoon salt and ¼ teaspoon pepper together. Coat chicken well in flour mixture and brown in frying pan with hot vegetable shortening. Sift 1½ cups flour, salt, and baking powder together. Beat eggs, milk, tabasco, and butter together. Add to dry ingredients and beat until smooth. Turn batter into well-greased 4-quart baking dish. When chicken is browned, place it in the batter, which will partially cover it. Bake in 375-degree oven for 45 to 60 minutes, or until batter is puffed and golden brown. If desired, may be served with giblet gravy.

Chicken Livers

1 pound chicken livers
1 cup hot coffee cream
2 tablespoons sherry
6 eggs, slightly beaten

½ teaspoon dried tarragon
   (optional)
Salt and pepper

Grind cooked livers and sieve to remove veins. Add cream, sherry, eggs, tarragon, salt and pepper to taste. Pour into buttered ring mold and set mold in a pan half filled with hot water. Bake until set in 325-degree oven (about 20 minutes). Unmold and fill center of ring with creamed mushrooms.

Chicken Pie

1 fryer (2 to 3 pounds)
1 teaspoon salt
⅛ teaspoon pepper
4 carrots
2 cups green peas

6 small spring onions
2 tablespoons flour
2 tablespoons water
1 cup chicken broth
1 cup milk

Cut chicken in pieces as for frying. Put in saucepan and cover with boiling water. Add 1 teaspoon salt and ⅛ teaspoon pepper. Heat to boiling; then simmer until tender or for about 45 minutes. Cut carrots in half lengthwise, then in 1 inch lengths. Cook with peas in small quantity of boiling salted water until tender. Cook onions in boiling water until tender, about 20 minutes. Drain vegetables.

(for biscuit dough)
2 cups sifted flour
3 teaspoons baking powder
½ teaspoon salt
4 tablespoons butter

1 cup (about) milk
½ teaspoon curry powder (optional)

Sift flour, baking powder, and ½ teaspoon salt into a mixing bowl. With 2 table knives or pastry blender cut in butter to form coarse crumbs. Add sufficient milk to form a soft dough. Roll out about two-thirds of dough on lightly floured board. Line bottom and sides of a 12 x 8 x 2″ baking dish up to the top edge. Trim off smoothly. Arrange pieces of cooked chicken over bottom of dish. Mix 2 table-spoons flour, 2 tablespoons water, and add to 1 cup chicken broth. Gradually add 1 cup milk, heat until thickened. Stir in cooked vege-tables and pour over chicken. Roll out remaining dough until rather thin and cut in 1-inch strips. Place criss-cross fashion over chicken and vegetables. Bake in a hot (400-degree) oven for about 30 min-utes or until the crust is light brown. Makes 6 servings.

Old Fashion Roast Chicken, à la Martha

1 4- to 5-pound roasting hen	1 small onion
1½ quarts water	Very small snip of hot red pepper
1 teaspoon vinegar	pod
1 teaspoon brown sugar	Salt and black pepper to taste

Put chicken with giblets on to cook, preferably in porcelain kettle (I like one with a pyrex top) with all of the seasonings and sufficient water to about half cover hen. Remove liver after about 15 minutes of simmering. Continue to simmer chicken until meat on drumstick is tender, about 1 hour. Remove chicken (and giblets, too, if you do not wish to use them for gravy) to open roasting pan. Turn chicken breast down and add sufficient stock for basting. Cook chicken in a 400-degree oven about 30 minutes, turning until it is browned nicely on all sides.

Chicken Scrapple

3½ cups chicken stock	¼ teaspoon white pepper
1 tablespoon flour	Dash of tabasco
1 cup white corn meal	2 cups finely chopped cooked
½ teaspoon salt	chicken

Bring half of stock to boiling point in a double boiler. Blend flour, corn meal, salt, pepper, and tabasco; mix with remaining cold stock. Slowly stir corn meal mixture into hot stock. Cook, stirring until mixture thickens. Continue cooking for 30 minutes. Stir in chicken. Pour into a well-greased loaf pan. Cool and refrigerate. When firm, cut in slices. Roll slices in flour and fry in bacon fat over moderate heat about 10 minutes, until brown, turning to brown on both sides. Serve with chicken gravy.

Roast Goose

When goose has been pinfeathered, singed, and washed after being drawn, sprinkle inside and out with salt; fasten legs together and tie down with cord across the back of goose. Place goose breast side down in open roasting pan and cook in 325-degree oven, allowing about 30 minutes a pound. When back is browned, turn and brown alternately on sides and breast. Cook until meat on drumstick is tender. I dislike the clamminess that putting dressing inside of poultry gives to it and prefer to season it by laying a stalk of celery, carrots, and chopped onions inside while bird is being roasted.

Roast Turkey

When turkey is ready to be cooked, put on in large kettle, adding sufficient cold water to about half cover the turkey. Season with salt and black pepper, 1 tablespoon of vinegar, 1 tablespoon brown sugar, 1 medium-size onion, and a small snip of hot-red-pepper pod. Add giblets, removing liver after about 15 minutes of simmering. Cook for about 30 minutes or until turkey is plumped out (which this parboiling does). Remove from kettle and drain. Fasten legs together and tie down with cord across back of turkey. Grease turkey thoroughly on outside with melted butter. Place turkey breast side down on a rack in open roasting pan (325-degree oven), adding a sufficient quantity of the broth for basting. Turn when back is browned. Turn and brown alternately on sides and breast. Roast until meat on drumstick is tender. Average roasting time for 10–12 pound turkey, 15 to 20 minutes a pound.

One of my old cookbooks calls the wishbone "merry thought" and says the turkey has none. My last Christmas turkey certainly had one, or a perfect facsimile. However, I do like the name "merry thought" rather better than the well-known name of "wishbone."

POULTRY DRESSING

Chestnut Dressing (with ham)

1 pound chestnuts (in the shell)
½ regular-size loaf bread
3 cups stock or water
½ cup cooked ham, finely chopped
¼ cup butter

½ stalk celery, finely chopped
2 medium onions, finely chopped
1 tablespoon parsley, finely chopped
Salt and black pepper to taste
Dash of tabasco

Boil chestnuts. Soak bread in 3 cups of water or stock. Add ham. Brown celery and onions lightly in butter. Remove from fire and add all other ingredients and blend thoroughly. Use as stuffing or accompaniment to poultry. If the latter, form into small cakes and bake uncovered in 350-degree oven until brown, about 30 minutes.

Chestnut Dressing (sufficient quantity for 12- or 15-pound turkey or goose, dressed)

16 chestnuts (in the shell)
3 pounds pork sausage
1 medium onion, finely chopped
Salt and black pepper

2 egg yolks
¼ cup brandy
¼ teaspoon grated nutmeg
¼ cup truffles, diced

Put chestnuts on to boil and cook until they are tender (using a kitchen fork to find out). Drain. Shell and skin chestnuts with sharp knife and mash with table fork. Heat together sausage and onion and cook until lightly browned, stirring as they cook. Remove from heat. Add chestnuts and remaining ingredients and blend well. Stuff bird if desired or form into cakes and bake until browned (about 30 minutes) in moderate oven (350 degrees).

Corn-Bread Dressing

2 cups white corn meal
1/4 teaspoon soda
2 cups buttermilk
2 tablespoons butter, melted
1 egg
Salt and pepper
Dash of tabasco

1/2 teaspoon salt
2 tablespoons butter
1 celery heart, finely chopped
1 large onion
1/2 cup stock
2 eggs

Make corn bread by combining corn meal, soda, buttermilk, melted butter, 1 egg; add salt, pepper, and tabasco to taste. Beat well and bake (in 350-degree oven) until brown or about 30 minutes. Crumble corn bread and add remaining ingredients. Bake separately (about 30 minutes in 350-degree oven) or stuff bird as desired. I use a 10″ iron frying pan if dressing is baked separately.

Ham and Nut Dressing for Roast Chicken

1/4 pound chopped boiled or baked
    ham
4 small onions
1 tablespoon butter

4 slices toasted bread with suffi-
    cient milk to moisten
1 teaspoon salt
1 jigger brandy
1/4 pound chopped pecan meats

Sauté onions in butter. Moisten toast with milk and then squeeze milk out. Add remaining ingredients to toast and mix thoroughly by hand. Stuff fowl as usual or form into cakes and bake separately in 350-degree oven about 30 minutes or until brown.

Poultry Dressing (with Brazil nuts)

2 cups toasted bread crumbs
1 cup fresh pork, cooked, ground
    (no fat)
4 white onions, finely chopped
1 tablespoon butter
Pinch of rosemary
Pinch of thyme

3 tablespoons finely chopped
    celery
1/2 cup mushrooms, finely chopped
Salt and pepper
Dash of tabasco
1 cup blanched Brazil nuts, finely
    chopped
Sherry (optional)

Mix bread crumbs and pork, adding onions with the butter in which they have been sautéed. Add rosemary, thyme, celery, and mushrooms; salt, pepper, and tabasco to taste. Add Brazil nuts. Add sherry if greater moisture is desired. Blend all ingredients thoroughly. Stuff fowl in the usual manner and bake by your favorite recipe. To shell Brazil nuts: Boil 5 minutes in 1 quart of water to which 1 tablespoon of salt has been added. Drain, cool, crack and remove shells; or roast in 400-degree oven about 20 minutes, then cool, crack and shell. To remove the brown skin, simmer 2 minutes in 1 quart of water to which 1½ teaspoons of soda have been added.

Poultry Dressing (*with corn*)

2 loaves (regular size) white
    bread with crusts removed
½ of the giblets, finely chopped
2 tablespoons poultry fat
¼ cup water
¼ pound fresh mushrooms
1 small onion (sautéed in butter)
1 tablespoon butter

1 cup celery, finely chopped
1 tablespoon chopped chives
1 cup canned corn (cream style)
Salt and pepper to taste
Dash of tabasco
4 eggs
Sherry

Simmer half of giblets with fat in about ¼ cup of water about 30 minutes. Cut bread in 1-inch cubes and put in large saucepan. Add mushrooms, cooked giblets, corn, onion (sautéed in butter), celery, and tablespoon chives, and other seasonings. Cook about 5 minutes, stirring to blend well. Allow to cool. Then mix in slightly beaten eggs. Moisten with sherry if too dry. Stuff fowl as usual.

Typical Poultry Dressing (*almost the best after all*)

1 cup finely chopped onion
2 cups finely chopped celery
½ giblets of the fowl, cooked and
    chopped
4 cups day-old bread crumbs

1 cup chicken or turkey stock
¼ cup butter
½ teaspoon salt
¼ teaspoon black pepper
Dash of tabasco

Sauté onions and celery in butter until lightly browned. Stir in finely cut up giblets. Remove from heat and add bread crumbs which have been mixed with stock. If mixture is too soft, press out some of the liquid. If too stiff, add small amount of stock. Shape into serving size cakes and bake until brown, or stuff fowl as usual. The quantities above are sufficient for 5 pounds of poultry. Multiply to suit size of bird.

Wild Rice Dressing

1 cup wild rice
Giblets
4 cups boiling water
1 teaspoon salt
3 tablespoons butter

2 tablespoons finely chopped onion
1 tablespoon finely chopped green pepper
1/8 teaspoon black pepper
Dash of tabasco

Wash rice thoroughly. Add giblets to water and salt, and simmer 20 minutes. Remove giblets from fire and chop fine. Cook rice in broth until tender and drain. Sauté onion and green pepper in butter and add to rice with giblets, black pepper, and tabasco. If too moist press out some of the liquid, or if too dry, add sufficient water. Stuff fowl as usual.

DUMPLINGS

Corn-Meal Dumplings

1 egg
1/4 cup milk
1/2 cup sifted flour

1/2 teaspoon salt
1 teaspoon baking powder
1/2 cup white corn meal

Beat egg and add to it the milk. Sift flour, baking powder, and salt together. Add corn meal. Add liquids to dry ingredients and drop by spoonfuls into boiling hot soup or stew. Cover tightly and cook 12 to 15 minutes.

Drop Dumplings

1 egg
1 cup flour
½ teaspoon baking powder

Pinch of salt
⅓ cup (about) milk
1 teaspoon melted butter

Beat egg. Sift flour, baking powder, and salt into egg. Stir well, adding sufficient milk to make batter; beat until smooth; add butter. Drop by tablespoonfuls into boiling stock. Cover and boil 10 minutes.

Egg and Cheese Dishes

Buckingham Eggs

6 slices of toast (with crusts removed)
Butter
Anchovy paste

6 eggs
Salt and pepper
Dash of tabasco
Grated cheese

Butter toast and spread thinly with anchovy paste. Beat eggs; season with salt, pepper, and tabasco to taste. Scramble eggs in butter until partially cooked. Pile eggs on toast and sprinkle generously with the grated cheese. Put in 450-degree oven for about 5 minutes or until cheese melts. Serves 6.

Deviled Eggs and Mushrooms

1 pound fresh mushrooms
Butter
12 hard-boiled eggs
½ teaspoon salt
¼ teaspoon black pepper

Dash of tabasco
2 cups white sauce
½ cup grated Cheddar cheese, sharp
Buttered bread crumbs

If there is time, my favorite method of hard-boiling eggs is to put them on in cold water in a saucepan and bring to a rolling boil; then turn off the heat and leave saucepan on the burner for about 20 minutes when the eggs will be hard-boiled, yet tender.

Sauté mushroom caps in butter and then chop them. Cut eggs lengthwise and remove yolks. Press yolks through a sieve. Blend some of the chopped mushrooms with yolks, and season with salt, pepper, and tabasco. Fill egg whites with mixture, pressing two halves together. Place stuffed eggs in a casserole and cover with white sauce to which has been added balance of chopped mushrooms. Mix equal amounts of bread crumbs and cheese together and sprinkle over the sauce. Bake in 400-degree oven until cheese and crumbs are browned. Serves 6.

Eggs à la King

4 tablespoons butter
1 cup sliced fresh mushrooms
2½ cups milk
4 tablespoons flour, sifted
1 teaspoon salt

⅛ teaspoon black pepper
Dash of tabasco
6 hard-boiled eggs, chopped
½ cup sliced stuffed olives

Melt butter in heavy saucepan over low heat. Add mushrooms; cover and allow to cook about 10 minutes. Stir once. Add 2 cups milk. Blend remaining milk, flour, salt, pepper, and tabasco. Add to mushrooms, stirring constantly until mixture is thickened. Add eggs and olives. Heat through. Serve in pastry shells or as desired. Garnish with parsley. Serves 6–8.

French Fried Deviled Eggs

6 eggs, hard-boiled
1 teaspoon Worcestershire sauce
1 teaspoon dry mustard
½ teaspoon salt
½ teaspoon white pepper
⅛ teaspoon tabasco

1 tablespoon India (sweet) relish
3 tablespoons mayonnaise
2 egg yolks
Sifted flour
Fine bread crumbs

Cut eggs lengthwise. Remove yolks and mash with table fork. Add Worcestershire sauce, dry mustard, salt, white pepper, tabasco, India relish, and mayonnaise. Blend well. Stuff whites and put eggs back together, holding with toothpicks. Dip eggs into 2 beaten egg yolks, then flour and bread crumbs. Fry in deep fat until golden brown. Drain eggs on brown paper and remove toothpicks. Serves 6. Parmesan Cheese does wonders for scrambled eggs. Sprinkle it on while eggs are cooking. Likewise tabasco added to eggs while you are beating them is a wonder worker as to flavor.

Omelet, *plain*

Eggs
Salted butter

Dash of tabasco

This is my favorite version of Madame Poulard's famous recipe: An omelet pan is desirable. Otherwise, choose your pan with the smoothest bottom. Beat eggs 10 minutes with wire whisk. In pre-heated pan, put sufficient salted butter (to which dash of tabasco has been added) to cover bottom of pan to depth of ¼ inch. When butter bubbles, pour in beaten eggs. As eggs cook, shake pan with rotary motion and run spatula around edges of pan. When omelet is golden at edges, remove to heated platter and fold over. Serve. Thorough beating of eggs, sufficient butter to prevent sticking to pan, and right degree of heat is the trio essential to this omelet's perfection.

Onion-Cheese Pasty

Pie shell, uncooked
2 medium-size onions
½ pound sharp Cheddar cheese

3 tablespoons milk
Dash of tabasco
Salt and pepper

Line 9-inch pie plate with pastry. Peel onions, slice thinly, and separate into rings. Arrange onion rings in even layer in pastry-lined pie plate. Slice cheese thinly and place in layer over onions. Sprinkle with milk to which tabasco has been added; then sprinkle with salt and pepper to taste. Trim pastry flush with edge of pie plate; fold pastry in so that top edge of fold is about two-thirds as high as pie plate. Flute around edge with fork. Bake in 400-degree oven for about 30 minutes or until cheese is melted and lightly browned. Serves 6 to 7.

Gay Nineties Rarebit

3 tablespoons butter
3 tablespoons flour, sifted
½ teaspoon salt
Dash of tabasco
½ cup milk
¼ cup sherry

1½ cups shredded sharp Cheddar
    cheese
1 cup beer or ale
6 pieces toast or English
    crumpets

Melt butter in large double boiler. Blend in flour and season with salt and tabasco. Pour milk in gradually, stirring constantly until mixture thickens, about 10 minutes. Remove from heat. Then add sherry slowly. Stir about 5 minutes or until thick and smooth. Add shredded cheese, stirring until melted and smooth. Stir in beer or ale slowly. If desired, reheat over low heat for a few minutes. Serve at once over crisp toast or well-toasted hot English crumpets. Serves 6–8.

Rancher's Omelet

6 slices bacon, diced
2 tablespoons onion, finely
   chopped
1 cup grated raw potato
6 eggs

½ teaspoon salt
⅛ teaspoon white pepper
Dash of tabasco
2 tablespoons minced parsley

Fry bacon until crisp. Remove from pan and drain. Leave 2 table-spoons of bacon grease. Add onion and sauté over low heat until soft. Add potatoes and cook until light brown. Beat eggs slightly and pour into pan. Add salt, pepper, and tabasco. As omelet cooks, lift up edges with spatula to let liquid egg mixture slide under. When firm, sprinkle omelet with crumbled crisp bacon and parsley. Fold over and serve. Serves 6 to 8.

Welsh Rarebit with Ale

1 tablespoon butter
1 pound sharp Cheddar cheese
Pinch of dry mustard

1 tablespoon chili sauce
Dash of tabasco
6 or 7 tablespoons ale

Melt butter, in chafing dish preferably; add grated cheese and sea-sonings. Blend well and add 1 tablespoon of ale at a time until 6 or 7 tablespoonfuls have been added, beating well after each addition. Cook 10 minutes; have slices of toast ready. Serve rarebit very hot. Serves 8–10.

Sea Foods

Crab Cutlets

2 pounds cooked crab meat
  (backfin if possible)
1 medium-size onion
¼ cup butter
1 cup flour
White stock

Parsley, finely minced
Salt and pepper
Dash of tabasco
1 egg
Bread crumbs

Chop onion very fine and sauté in the butter until soft. Strain out
the onion and add flour to the butter very gradually. Next add sufficient white stock to make a thick sauce. Season to taste with salt
and pepper, dash of tabasco, and parsley. Add crab meat and chill.
Shape crab mixture into cutlets; dip in slightly beaten egg, then roll
in bread crumbs. Fry in deep fat (375–385 degrees) until golden
brown. (If you have no fat thermometer, test heat with bread. One-

inch bread cubes brown in about 40 seconds at these temperatures.) Serve with the following sauce: Heat 2 cups white stock in sauce-pan with ½ bay leaf, ¼ teaspoon celery seed, 2 tablespoons apple cider vinegar and ¼ cup butter. Simmer for 5 minutes, then strain to remove bay leaf and celery seed. Mix 2 tablespoons flour with sufficient water (about ½ cup) to make a thin paste. Add to stock, stirring constantly. Cook about 5 minutes, or until sauce thickens. *The white stock is made as follows:*

1 veal knuckle	½ teaspoon thyme
1 medium-size onion	½ bay leaf
1 medium-size carrot	1 teaspoon salt

Place all ingredients in soup kettle and cover with water. Simmer slowly about 3 hours, adding more water if needed. Strain at end of cooking period.

Stuffed Crabs, à la Creole

1 dozen large crabs, cooked and cleaned or ½-pound can of crab meat	Hot milk or water as needed
	6 slices toast, crumbled
	¼ teaspoon grated nutmeg
¼ cup finely minced onion	Salt and pepper
1 clove garlic, minced to a paste	Dash of tabasco
¾ cup minced green pepper	1 small bay leaf
¼ cup butter	Cracker crumbs

Pick crab meat from bodies and claws. Save empty crab shells. Sauté onions, garlic, and green pepper in butter over low heat. Add crab meat and cook until golden. Add sufficient hot milk or water to half fill the pan (appropriate size, about 1½ quarts). Add crumbled toast, nutmeg, salt and pepper to taste, tabasco, and bay leaf. Cook until thick, stirring constantly. Remove bay leaf. Fill crab shells with the mixture and top with cracker crumbs. Bake in 325-degree oven for 15 minutes. If crab shells are not available, bake the mixture in individual ramekins or stuff green peppers with it. Makes 6 servings.

Crab Meat on Wild Rice

1½ cups raw wild rice	¼ teaspoon white pepper
3 tablespoons butter	Dash of tabasco
2 tablespoons flour	2 tablespoons sherry
1 cup coffee cream	2½ cups fresh crab meat
½ teaspoon salt	Parsley

Wash rice in several waters and soak overnight. Drain and cook in boiling, salted water to cover until tender, about 30 minutes. Drain and keep hot. Melt butter and blend in flour. Add cream gradually, stirring constantly. Cook over low heat until thickened or about 10 minutes. Add salt, pepper, tabasco, sherry, and crab meat. Simmer for 5 minutes. Season rice and spread on a hot platter and cover with creamed crab meat. Garnish with parsley. Serves 6 to 8.

Oyster Sausage (From *Housekeeping in Old Virginia.* Copied verbatim. Copyrighted 1879).

1 pint of raw oysters with ¼ pound veal and ¼ pound suet. Mix with bread crumbs, and pound all in a mortar. Season with salt and pepper, adding an egg, well beaten. Make into cakes like pork sausage.—Mrs. E.

Deviled Oysters on Half Shell

1 pint oysters	½ teaspoon salt
3 shallots, finely chopped or 1 teaspoon minced green onions	Dash of tabasco
	½ teaspoon dry mustard
1 tablespoon butter	1 teaspoon Worcestershire sauce
2 tablespoons flour	3 mushroom caps, finely chopped
½ cup milk	½ teaspoon minced parsley
¼ cup coffee cream	1 egg yolk
⅛ teaspoon nutmeg	Buttered cracker crumbs

Wash and chop oysters. Cook shallots (or onions) in butter 3 minutes over low heat. Add flour and blend. Add milk and cream and stir until slightly thickened. Add oysters and remaining ingredients (except egg yolk and crumbs), and simmer for 12 minutes. Stir in egg yolk. Put mixture in deep halves of oyster shells, cover with buttered crumbs and bake at 400 degrees for 15 to 20 minutes. 6 servings.

Scalloped Oysters

2 cups (1 pint) whole oysters
2 cups (1 pint) oysters, coarsely
  chopped
1 pint coffee cream
½ lemon, juice, and grated peel
Pinch of mace

Salt and pepper
Dash of tabasco
1 teaspoon flour
Egg yolk
Bread crumbs

Add cream, lemon juice and peel, salt and pepper to taste, mace, tabasco, and flour to chopped oysters. Cook in double boiler until sauce is slightly thickened, or about 15 minutes. Dry the whole oysters and dip in egg yolk, then in fine bread crumbs. Put whole oysters in 2 layers in bottom of baking dish. Cover with chopped oyster mixture. If more than 2 layers, the middle layer is apt not to cook as quickly as the other 2 layers. Bake in 325-degree oven for about 30 minutes.

Baked Sea Food au Gratin

½ pound butter
1 medium-size onion
1 green pepper
1 cup flour
1-pound lump crab meat
½ pound scallops
1 pound shrimp
½ pound flounder

3 cups hot milk
¼ pound sharp Cheddar cheese
1 teaspoon Worcestershire sauce
Parmesan cheese
1 tablespoon vinegar
Salt and pepper
Dash of tabasco

Chop onion and pepper. Melt ¼ pound butter in saucepan; add pepper and onion and sauté for 5 minutes. Add about ½ cup of flour and cook 10 minutes. Add crab meat and blend well. Form the mixture into cakes about the size of sausage cakes. Boil scallops, shrimp, and flounder meat, and save stock for sauce. Put ¼ pound butter in saucepan. When melted, add ½ cup flour and cook for 5 minutes. Add 3 cups hot milk stirring all the while. Add stock from shrimp, scallops, and flounder (if less than 1 cup add water to make that amount) and cook for 10 minutes. Add grated cheddar cheese, dash of tabasco, 1 teaspoon Worcestershire sauce, 1 tablespoon of vinegar, and salt and pepper to taste. Put scallops, shrimp, and fish in sauce. Stir gently. Place crab cakes in casserole. Pour mixture over them. Sprinkle grated Parmesan cheese on top. Brush lightly with melted butter. Place in 350-degree oven for 15 minutes. Serves 10–12.

Sea Food Newburg

1 pint oysters
½ pound fresh crab meat
½ pound cooked shrimp
½ pound butter

1 pint milk
Salt and pepper to taste
Dash of tabasco
½ cup sherry

Make sauce of 1 tablespoon butter and flour in double boiler, blending well. Add milk and stir mixture until thick. Remove from fire. Put remainder of butter in a saucepan and allow to reach boiling point. Add sea food and seasonings and sauté 5 minutes. Add white sauce and wine. Serves 10–12.

Shad Roe

Cover shad roe with boiling water and add to it 1 tablespoon vinegar and 1 tablespoon of salt. Cook 30 minutes, simmering slowly. Drain, cover with cold water for 5 minutes. Drain and sauté in butter or bacon grease until brown. Frequent burns (to the cook, from spattering grease, that is) are apt to result if the roe is not parboiled in advance as above. This method keeps the roe from breaking, too. Some cooks prefer to wrap the roe in wax paper, twisting the ends, and frying until roe is brown.

Shad Roe au Gratin

Parboil shad roe 20 minutes. Skin and remove all veins. Mash roe very fine, mixing in 2 thin slices of garlic, finely minced. Make sauce of ½ cup white wine, ½ cup light cream, ¼ teaspoon powdered sweet marjoram, ¼ teaspoon powdered rosemary, pepper and salt to taste, dash of tabasco, and 1 teaspoon of finely chopped parsley. Blend ingredients well. Pour sauce into shad roe and blend thoroughly. Fill shells or ramekin dishes with roe mixture. Pour melted butter over each. Sprinkle with grated Melba toast, add light dusting of Parmesan cheese. Run under broiler until surface is golden brown.

Baked Shad with Roe Stuffing

1 large roe shad	2 cups water
2 tablespoons vinegar	½ cup lemon juice
½ cup finely chopped onion	2 tablespoons Worcestershire
½ cup butter	sauce
3 eggs	Salt and pepper
1 cup bread crumbs	Dash of tabasco

Boil roe for about 20 minutes in 2 cups of water to which 2 tablespoons of vinegar have been added. Remove skin and mash roe. Sauté the onion in butter slowly and add to roe; add beaten eggs and bread crumbs. Salt and pepper to taste. Put stuffing into the shad and truss. Place in baking pan. Add 2 cups of water to which has been added the lemon juice, Worcestershire sauce, and tabasco. Bake 30 to 40 minutes in 350-degree oven. Baste. Serves 6.

Steamed Shrimp

Using a steamer or large saucepan with a wire rack, pour in 2 bottles of beer for each pound of shrimp. After boiling has begun, drop in unshelled shrimp. Cover tightly and steam for about 20 minutes. Remove shrimp to platters and provide dishes for melted butter in which to dip shrimp which the individual diner peels as he eats. There is no beery taste as the alcohol evaporates in cooking.

Vegetables

Baked Bananas

3 tablespoons butter
6 tablespoons sugar
3 tablespoons lemon juice

6 bananas
3 tablespoons rum or sherry

Melt butter. Add sugar and lemon juice and stir until well blended. Then remove from fire. Remove skins and place bananas in shallow baking dish. Sprinkle with rum or sherry. Then pour on butter sauce and place in 350-degree oven for 30 minutes. During baking, baste several times with butter sauce. Serve from baking dish.

I enjoy bananas baked in their skins and served hot around roast beef. Bake in greased shallow pan in a moderate oven (365 to 375 degrees) for about 20 minutes.

Boston Baked Beans

2 cups navy beans
½ pound lean salt pork
¼ cup tomato catsup
2 tablespoons country sorghum
    or New Orleans molasses
1 teaspoon Worcestershire sauce

½ teaspoon dry mustard
¼ teaspon black pepper
1 small onion
Small snip of red pepper pod
Salt (if salt pork does not provide
    sufficient)

Wash beans and soak overnight. In the morning drain and cover with fresh water and allow beans to simmer with pork (rind down), sorghum and other seasonings until noon. Then put beans and liquid in bean pot, score pork rind in squares or diamonds and turn right side up so rind shows just above beans. Let beans bake, covered, all afternoon in 350-degree oven. Add a little boiling water from time to time if they become dry. Remove cover and let beans get dry and brown on top in the last hour of baking.

Beets in Orange Sauce

8 to 10 beets, sliced
1 small onion, grated
1 tablespoon vinegar
3 tablespoons brown sugar

1 tablespoon melted butter
1 orange, juice and grated rind
Salt and pepper to taste
Dash of tabasco

Boil beets just long enough to peel easily. Then slice them and mix all ingredients and place in saucepan. Cover tightly and simmer for 15 minutes or until beets are tender. Serve at once.

Broccoli Bake

4 ounces cream cheese
½ cup milk
¼ cup sherry
1 package frozen broccoli spears
½ cup water

½ teaspoon salt
4 hard-boiled eggs, cut in halves
1 4-ounce can of pimientos, cut
    in large pieces
¼ cup cracker crumbs

Melt cream cheese in milk over low heat. Remove from heat. Add sherry. Cook broccoli until tender in water to which salt has been added; drain. Pour half of the cheese-milk-sherry mixture into a casserole. Lay the broccoli in it and place the halves of eggs between spears. Top with pimiento pieces. Add remaining sauce and sprinkle with crumbs. Bake in 325-degree oven for 25 to 30 minutes. 4 servings.

Broccoli with Parmesan Cheese

Cook broccoli until tender, drain, and prepare the following sauce: Put 1 cup of white sauce into a double boiler and heat it, adding ½ pound of grated Parmesan cheese. When it is thoroughly heated, add 1 egg yolk and a dash of tabasco. Grease a baking dish and put several tablespoonfuls of the sauce in the dish. Put broccoli in the dish and cover with bread crumbs and the white sauce-Parmesan cheese mixture. Put in 350-degree oven for 20 to 30 minutes, or until crumbs brown and cheese melts.

Brussels Sprouts with Chestnuts

1 quart Brussels sprouts
2 tablespoons butter
2 tablespoons flour
1 cup water (in which sprouts were cooked)

1 chicken bouillon cube
1 pound cooked chestnuts
2 tablespoons chopped pimiento
Dash of tabasco

Boil sprouts in salted water until tender. Make sauce from butter, flour, and water. Add bouillon cube and blend thoroughly. Combine sauce, Brussels sprouts, cooked and shelled chestnuts, pimiento, and tabasco.

Sour Cream Cabbage

4 tablespoons butter
4 cups grated cabbage
1 teaspoon salt

1 tablespoon sugar
Dash of tabasco
½ cup sour cream

Melt butter in skillet; add grated cabbage and cook over low heat about 20 minutes, stirring constantly. Add salt, sugar, tabasco, and sour cream. Stir cream through cabbage until the mixture is thoroughly heated, but do not boil. Serve hot. 4 servings.

Carrot Balls

2 cups cooked carrots, sieved
1½ cups bread crumbs
1 cup sharp Cheddar cheese, shredded

1 egg white
Salt and pepper to taste
Dash of tabasco
Corn flakes

Combine carrots, bread crumbs, and cheese. Fold in stiffly beaten egg white. Add seasonings. Form into 10 balls and roll in finely crushed corn flakes. Place on greased baking sheet or in shallow biscuit pan. Bake in 375-degree oven about 30 minutes or until brown.

Cauliflower au Gratin

1 small head cauliflower
2 tablespoons mayonnaise
Dash of tabasco
2 cups medium white sauce

1 cup grated sharp Cheddar cheese
Paprika

Separate cauliflower into flowerets. Cook covered in a small amount of boiling water until just tender (about 10 minutes) and drain. Place in a greased shallow casserole. Blend mayonnaise and tabasco with the white sauce and pour over cauliflower. Sprinkle with cheese. Then dust lightly with paprika. Bake in a moderate oven, about 350 degrees, until top is a light brown, about 20 minutes. 5 to 6 servings.

Cauliflower in Pimiento Cups

Break cauliflower into flowerets and steam over salted water until barely tender. Season with butter. Use whole pimientos as cups and fill with the flowerets. Put in oven for a few minutes just before serving, until heated through. Sprinkle with paprika and garnish with parsley bits.

Chestnut Croquettes

1 cup chestnut meal or 1 cup raw
   chestnuts, grated
2 egg yolks
2 tablespoons heavy cream

½ teaspoon sugar
¼ teaspoon salt
Bread crumbs

Blend first five ingredients thoroughly. Shape into desired croquette form and roll in fine bread crumbs. Fry until brown on all sides in hot fat and drain. Serve hot with lamb chops or other meat dishes.

Chestnuts en Casserole

3 cups cooked *shelled* chestnuts
3 cups chicken stock
2 tablespoons butter

1½ tablespoons flour
Salt and pepper
Dash of tabasco

Cut a slit ½" deep in each chestnut. For each cup of chestnuts use a teaspoon of butter. Cook the chestnuts in a frying pan for 5 minutes, tossing them, and then place the pan in the oven for 5 minutes. The shells and skins are then easily peeled off with a paring knife. Melt remaining tablespoon of butter in casserole and blend in flour, with as much chicken stock as may be required to make a thin paste. Add chestnuts, pour in rest of the stock, add salt, pepper and tabasco and bake in 325-degree oven about 3 hours.

Fried Celery Hearts

3 tablespoons flour
1 egg
1 cup milk
3 bunches celery hearts

Chicken stock or water
1 cup fine dry bread crumbs
Salt and white pepper to taste
Dash of tabasco

Blend flour and slightly beaten egg. Add milk gradually, beating after each addition. Wash celery hearts thoroughly and cut into quarters. Cook in chicken stock or water to cover for 10 minutes and drain. Dip celery into batter, then into bread crumbs. Fry in deep fat (375 degrees) until golden brown.

Corn Pudding

1 tablespoon melted butter
1 tablespoon flour
1 teaspoon salt
1 tablespoon sugar
⅛ teaspoon white pepper
Few drops of tabasco
1½ cups milk

1 teaspoon scraped onion
1 tablespoon chopped pimiento
2 eggs, slightly beaten
2 cups corn, preferably fresh
   (Frozen or canned corn may
   be substituted. If canned corn
   is used, drain before mixing.)

Combine melted butter, flour, salt, sugar, pepper, and tabasco. Add milk slowly, stirring until smooth. Cook until thick or about 10 minutes, stirring constantly. Remove from fire, add onion, pimiento, eggs, and corn, and mix well. Turn into greased baking dish. Set dish in pan of hot water and bake in 325-degree oven 1 hour or until set, and slightly brown on top.

Rosette Corn Pudding

3 tablespoons chopped onion
2 tablespoons butter
1 tablespoon flour
½ cup milk
3 eggs, slightly beaten

1 #1 can cream style corn or corn
   cut from 3 large ears
Salt and pepper to taste
4 firm but ripe tomatoes

Sauté onions in butter until soft. Blend in flour; add milk gradually, stirring constantly until thick and smooth. Stir slowly into beaten eggs; add corn; season. Wash and core tomatoes. Make 3 cuts from blossom end to within ¾ inch of stem end. Place in shallow 6-cup baking dish and open segments. Pour corn mixture around tomatoes. Place dish in pan of hot water; bake in moderate oven (350 degrees) about 1 hour or until corn mixture is set.

Baked Cucumbers

6 cucumbers
4 slices cubed bacon
1 sliver garlic
1 green pepper, finely chopped
1 #1 can whole kernel corn or corn from 3 large ears

6 medium-size tomatoes, peeled
Salt and pepper to taste
Dash of tabasco
Sharp Cheddar cheese, grated
Bread crumbs

Cut cucumbers in half, lengthwise, and hollow out the seeds. Fry bacon bits. Add sliver of garlic, green pepper, corn, and tomatoes and cook until rather thick, or about 20 minutes. Add seasonings. Strain off the juice and stuff cucumbers with mixture, cover with cheese and crumbs and bake in 325-degree oven for 1½ hours.

French Fried Cucumbers

Cucumbers
1 egg
Salt and pepper to taste

Few drops of tabasco
Bread crumbs

Peel cucumbers and slice in quarter-inch slices. Soak in cold salted water for 30 minutes. Beat egg slightly and add seasonings and 1 tablespoon of cold water. Dip cucumber slices in egg mixture, and then in crumbs, and fry in deep, hot fat until golden brown.

Eggplant High Hat

1 medium-size eggplant
1 cup finely crushed cracker crumbs
½ cup coffee cream
Dash of tabasco

Shortening
Onions
Tomatoes
Sharp Cheddar cheese
Salt and pepper

Peel and cut 6 half-inch-thick crosswise slices from eggplant. Dip each slice in crumbs, then in cream to which dash of tabasco has been added; then in crumbs again. Sauté eggplant in frying pan in hot, bubbling shortening until golden brown, or about 15 minutes. Remove slices from pan; place on baking sheet or in shallow biscuit pan. On top of each slice of eggplant put first a slice of onion, then a slice of tomato and top with a slice of cheese. Sprinkle each with salt and pepper to taste. Bake in 350-degree oven about 25 minutes or until cheese has melted and is slightly browned.

Eggplant Medley

1 eggplant
1 teaspoon vinegar
½ green pepper, finely chopped
2 tablespoons minced onion
2 tablespoons butter
2 medium-size tomatoes
1½ cups cooked rice

½ cup sharp Cheddar cheese, grated
Salt and pepper to taste
Dash of tabasco
Dry bread crumbs
Butter, for dotting the top of Medley

Peel and cut eggplant in finger-size pieces; cover with cold salted water for 30 minutes. Cover drained eggplant pieces with boiling salted water to which the vinegar has been added. Parboil until tender, approximately 20 minutes. Drain. In a frying pan melt 2 tablespoons butter. Add green pepper and onion and sauté until partly cooked, or about 20 minutes. Then add peeled and chopped tomatoes and leave over heat until these are slightly cooked, or for about 15 minutes. Add tomato mixture to drained, cooked and partly mashed eggplant, rice, and cheese. Add seasonings. Put in greased baking dish. Top with crumbs and dot with butter. Put in 350-degree oven for about 30 minutes, or until top of Medley is golden brown.

Eggplant Stuffed

1 eggplant
¼ cup chopped onion
3 tablespoons butter
½ cup bread crumbs

1½ cups corn, canned whole kernel or fresh
Salt and pepper
Dash of tabasco

Cut eggplant in half lengthwise. Boil about 10 minutes. Scoop out centers and chop fine. Sauté onion in butter until soft; mix with eggplant centers, the bread crumbs, corn; salt, pepper and tabasco to taste. Stuff the eggplant shells, dot with butter and bake in 425-degree oven about 20 minutes.

Hopping John

2 cups black-eyed peas	2 tablespoons butter
¼ pound lean salt pork	Salt and pepper to taste
2 cups cooked rice	Dash of tabasco

Wash peas and soak overnight. Drain. Add sliced salt pork. Cover with water and cook until tender but not mushy (about 30 minutes). To the small amount of liquid which should remain, add rice, butter, and seasonings. Simmer 15 minutes longer, covered.

I understand Hopping John is served traditionally in the Deep South on New Year's Day to insure good luck throughout the year. In Virginia the black-eyed peas must be cooked with hog jowl and no rice is added. My version goes about like this:

½ cured hog jowl	Salt and pepper to taste
2 cups black-eyed peas	Small snip of hot red pepper pod
1 small onion	

Wash peas and soak overnight. Scrub and trim jowl thoroughly. Put on to cook in kettle with water to cover. Parboil until tender or about 1 hour. Then add peas, onion, and seasonings. Cook until peas are done or the liquid is thick and soupy; about 1 hour.

French Fried Onions

Slice large peeled Bermuda onions about ¼ inch thick. Separate into rings. Soak rings 15 minutes or more in fresh or undiluted evaporated milk. Drain slightly. Beat 1 egg, add ½ cup milk. Roll rings in flour, then egg mixture and into bread crumbs. Gently shake to remove surplus crumbs. Heat shortening in deep-fat fryer to 375 degrees. Fry from 2 to 3 minutes or until golden brown.

Stuffed Onions

6 large mild onions
1 cup chopped cooked chicken
   livers
1 cup chopped cooked ham

Butter
Salt and pepper
Dash of tabasco
Sherry

Peel onions and parboil in boiling salted water until just tender or about 30 minutes. Drain and scoop out centers, leaving a good wall. Brush insides with melted butter and sprinkle with salt and pepper. Sauté livers and ham until hot in butter to which salt, pepper, and tabasco have been added. Fill onion shells with the mixture; brush melted butter over top and set onions in a shallow baking dish with cover. Bake in 325-degree oven until tender or about 30 minutes. Anoint with a small quantity of sherry before serving.

Baked Peanuts

2 cups whole, shelled, raw peanuts
2 teaspoons salt
1 cup tomatoes, peeled and
   chopped (fresh or canned)
2 tablespoons minced onion
2 tablespoons molasses
2 tablespoons brown sugar

$\frac{1}{4}$ teaspoon black pepper
$\frac{1}{2}$ teaspoon Worcestershire sauce
$\frac{1}{8}$ teaspoon tabasco
2 tablespoons tomato catsup
6 strips bacon or streak o' lean-
   streak o' fat salt pork
$\frac{1}{4}$ teaspoon celery seed
$\frac{3}{4}$ teaspoon curry powder

Soak peanuts overnight. Add salt and steam until peanuts are tender. Put peanuts in greased baking dish. Blend all other ingredients except bacon (or pork) and pour over peanuts. Arrange bacon or pork on top of peanut mixture. Bake in 350-degree oven about 45 minutes.

Peas Epicurean

4 strips bacon
½ large Bermuda onion, chopped
1 cup canned or fresh mushrooms
1 tablespoon flour
1 cup heavy cream

Salt and freshly ground pepper
Worcestershire sauce and Ac'cent
¼ cup sherry
1 #2 can green peas
(2½ cupfuls)

Chop raw bacon into pieces and sauté with onion until brown. If fresh mushrooms are used, these should be sautéed at the same time. Add flour and cream, stirring constantly over low flame. After sauce has thickened and is smooth, add seasonings and sherry and mushrooms (if canned ones are used). Fold peas gently into mixture. Serves 6.

Welsh Rabbit Peppers

6 medium-size green peppers
1 pound sharp Cheddar cheese
2 pimientos
1 cup soft bread crumbs
1 cup milk

¼ teaspoon dry mustard
½ teaspoon grated onion
Salt and pepper to taste
1 tablespoon melted butter

Grind cheese and pimientos together. Soak bread crumbs in milk for a few minutes. Squeeze out excess liquid. Add seasonings and combine all ingredients. Cut tops off pepper and remove seeds and white fibrous part. Fill with the cheese mixture and place in a shallow pan. Add sufficient water to cover the bottom of the pan. Bake in a moderate (375-degree) oven about 30 minutes.

Potato Apples

3 cups hot mashed potatoes
½ cup hot milk
Salt and pepper to taste
Dash of tabasco

½ cup grated sharp Cheddar cheese
1 egg
Fine bread crumbs

Blend all ingredients thoroughly except egg and bread crumbs; then place by tablespoonfuls on a platter. Refrigerate until cold, then shape into balls. Roll in egg, then in bread crumbs. Fry in hot bubbling fat until lightly browned. Insert the blossom end of a clove in one side and stem end in opposite side to represent apples. Add paprika on one side if blush is desired. Serve hot.

New Potatoes in Sauce

Combine cooked new potatoes with very small boiled white onions in a sherried cheese sauce, made by adding grated sharp Cheddar cheese and a generous measure of sherry to basic cream or white sauce. Turn into shallow casserole. Sprinkle with toasted bread crumbs, and dot with butter. Bake in moderate oven (325–350 degrees) about 20 minutes to blend flavors. Garnish with parsley when serving.

Scalloped Potatoes

6 to 8 medium-size potatoes	1½ teaspoons salt
1 medium-size onion	¼ teaspoon white pepper
2 tablespoons butter	Dash of tabasco
2 tablespoons flour	2 cups milk

Peel potatoes and onion and slice medium thin. Place in casserole in alternate layers. Melt butter in saucepan over medium heat. Add flour, stir until smooth. Add salt, pepper, tabasco, and milk, stirring constantly until thickened. Remove from heat and pour over potatoes. Bake uncovered in preheated 350-degree oven for 1 hour. Serves 6.

Sliced Potatoes

Peel and thinly slice potatoes. Wrap in heavy foil, adding salt, pepper, a little cream, and sharp Cheddar cheese, grated. Bake in moderate (350–375 degree) oven until potatoes are tender (approximately 30 minutes).

Baked Sweet Potatoes and Pippins

6 medium-size sweet potatoes
  or yams
4 tart apples, peeled and cored
½ cup dark brown sugar

¼ teaspoon mace
¼ teaspoon nutmeg
¼ cup butter
½ cup apple cider or apple juice

Cook potatoes in jackets in boiling salted water to cover until tender. Peel; cut into ½-inch slices. Cut apples into ¼-inch slices. Place potatoes and apples in alternate layers in buttered 2-quart baking dish. Sprinkle with sugar, mace, and nutmeg. Dot with butter. Pour in apple cider or juice. Bake in 350-degree oven for about 1 hour or until apples are tender. 6 to 8 servings.

French Fried Rice

Heat oil in a deep fat fryer. Fill fine mesh basket, kitchen strainer, or sieve with cooled, cooked rice. Fry in deep fat (375 degrees), until light brown, for about 3 minutes. Remove and drain on paper toweling.

Wild Rice Croquettes

Wash 1 cup wild rice in several waters and soak overnight. Drain and cook in 3 cups chicken stock in double boiler, stirring occasionally until liquid is absorbed or about 30 minutes. Beat 4 egg yolks; add 1 thin slice finely chopped garlic, 1 teaspoon onion juice, 1 tablespoon each very finely chopped parsley and chives; salt and pepper to taste and dash of tabasco. Add the mixture to rice, together with 2 parboiled chicken livers finely mashed with a table fork. Chill thoroughly and form into croquettes. Dip in beaten egg and milk. Then roll in sieved dry bread crumbs. Refrigerate croquettes until ready for use (at least 2 hours). Fry in deep hot fat (390 degrees) until golden brown. Drain on absorbent paper and serve hot.

Wild Rice with Chicken Livers

Wash 1 cup wild rice in several waters and soak overnight. Drain and cook in 1 quart of boiling salted water until tender (from 40 to 60 minutes). Sauté ½ pound chicken livers in ¼ cup butter with 1 onion, finely chopped, pinch of thyme, pinch of marjoram, salt and pepper to taste, and dash of tabasco. Drain rice in colander. Blend well with chicken livers and serve hot.

1 teaspoonful of oil in white or brown rice will keep grains separate and prevent boiling over.

Snaps (with "Old" ham bone or Smithfield ham bone)

2 pounds snaps (string beans) (preferably Kentucky Wonder variety)
1 ham bone, cooked

½ teaspoon salt
Small snip of hot red pepper pod
1 teaspoon sugar
Water

Put ham bone in large saucepan or kettle of water. Bring to boil. String snaps and break in desired lengths. Add with seasonings to ham bone in the boiling water. Cook briskly for 2 or 3 hours or until water has cooked out. If water cooks out before two hours, add more hot water. Remove ham bone from snaps when all meat can be pushed off with a spoon.

I can't work up any enthusiasm for snaps cooked in any other way. If I have to use a substitute for the ham bone, I fry either a few pieces of breakfast bacon or streak o' lean-streak o' fat salt pork and then add the grease and the bacon or pork to the snaps, but that heavenly flavor a ham bone gives to snaps is not there.

Texas Stuffed Tomatoes

6 ripe, unpeeled tomatoes
1 cup cooked lima beans
½ cup fresh bread cubes
2 tablespoons of chopped onion
½ cup of sharp Cheddar cheese, grated

1 egg, beaten
½ teaspoonful sugar
½ teaspoonful salt
Sprinkle of black pepper

Scoop out insides of the tomatoes. Chop and combine with the other ingredients. Stuff the tomato shells and set in a shallow pan with about 1 inch of boiling water in the bottom of the pan. Bake in a moderate (about 365-degree) oven for 15 to 20 minutes.

Vegetable Casserole

8 small new potatoes
8 baby carrots
1 small cauliflower (broken into flowerets)
1 cup green peas
1 cup baby lima beans

½ pound sharp Cheddar cheese; sliced
2 cups medium cream sauce
Celery and onion broth
1 tablespoon grated cheese
Parsley, chopped

Cook vegetables separately until barely done. Drain well. Mix and place in casserole. Add sliced cheese to hot cream sauce and stir until melted. Simmer together 3 stalks of celery and 2 small onions in 1 cup of water for ½ hour to provide the broth. Strain. Mix broth into sauce and pour over vegetables. Place casserole in 350-degree oven for about 30 minutes, or until thoroughly heated. Sprinkle lightly with grated cheese and garnish with parsley. 8 servings.

Wax Beans au Gratin

2 #1 cans cut yellow wax beans
2 tablespoons butter
1 tablespoon brown sugar

1 cup sharp Cheddar cheese, grated
White sauce

Drain about half of juice from beans and sauté over low heat in butter and brown sugar until dry, or about 20 minutes. Combine with 1 cup white sauce flavored with ½ cup of cheese. Place in buttered casserole and cover the top with remaining ½ cup of cheese. Bake 20 minutes in 350-degree oven. 4 or 5 servings.

Zucchini

Peel 4 medium-size zucchini and slice crosswise in quarter-inch slices. Put 1 tablespoonful of olive oil in frying pan over moderate heat. Add 1 sliced clove of garlic. Sauté garlic until brown. Remove before adding other ingredients. Add zucchini, 2 medium-size tomatoes (quartered), ½ onion, (minced), and a few very thin slivers of green pepper. Add ½ teaspoonful of sugar, salt and pepper to taste, and dash of tabasco. Cover and cook slowly about 30 minutes, until zucchini and pepper are tender. 5 servings.

Salads and Salad Dressings

Chicken Salad

2 cups chopped boiled chicken
   (light meat is generally
   considered preferable)
1 cup finely chopped celery
¼ large sour pickle, finely
   chopped

Mayonnaise
2 hard-boiled eggs (mashed
   with table fork) or may be
   quartered and used as a
   garnish

Blend all ingredients well except eggs. I like these added after
mayonnaise has been added.

107

Many Virginia hostesses well known for the excellence of the food served in their homes prefer the following dressing, generally used in an older day for chicken salad.

Yolks of 2 hard-boiled eggs, finely mashed
1 teaspoon dry mustard
1 tablespoon sugar
2 tablespoons flour
1 cup chicken broth (from which fat has been removed)

1 tablespoon olive oil
1 tablespoon chicken fat or 2 tablespoons butter
Salt and black pepper to taste
3 tablespoons mayonnaise

Blend seasonings with egg yolks. Add flour. To this add chicken broth. Put olive oil and chicken fat (or butter) in a saucepan. When hot but not boiling, add broth and seasoned mixture. Cook over low temperature until consistency of mayonnaise. Chill and add mayonnaise. Add whites of the 2 hard-boiled eggs, finely chopped, if desired.

Combination Salad

2 envelopes plain gelatin
½ cup cold water
⅔ cup sugar
2 cups boiling water
1 teaspoon salt
½ cup apple cider vinegar

Juice of 1 lemon
1 cup finely chopped cabbage
2 cups finely chopped celery
2 pimientos, shredded
½ cup nut meats, chopped

Soak gelatin in cold water; then in boiling water dissolve soaked gelatin and sugar. Add salt, vinegar, and lemon juice; arrange cut vegetables and nuts in layers in a mold; fill mold with gelatin mixture by pouring into a spoon held firmly on top of layers and allowing it to trickle down. Refrigerate until firm. Cut in cubes with a warm knife, or cut with a cutter and serve on lettuce with mayonnaise.

Fruit Salad

Use favorite mixture of fruits on lettuce, garnished with water cress. For dressing use:

¼ cup sugar
¼ cup lemon juice
¼ cup sherry
Few grains of salt

2 tablespoonfuls of minced mint leaves
Dash of tabasco

Blend all ingredients for dressing until sugar is dissolved. Pass at table to be added to each serving.

Lulu Paste

1 pound sharp Cheddar cheese
1 small onion
1 4-ounce can pimientos
½ cup tomato catsup

1 pinch dry mustard
A little chili sauce (optional)
1 cup mayonnaise

Grind cheese, onion, and pimientos in food grinder. Add other ingredients and stir until well mixed. Store in screw-top jar in icebox. This is considered an heirloom recipe in Richmond. It is a very delicious spread.

Onion-Orange Salad

Large oranges   Large Bermuda onions

Blend salad oil with vinegar, salt, pepper, and tabasco (just a dash of this) in the proportions that please you. Chill salad ingredients thoroughly and serve one slice each of onion and orange on lettuce or other greens with salad dressing. To peel oranges easily, leave them in scalding hot water for 5 minutes.

Potato Salad

Onions being a favorite addition of mine to most foods, perhaps it is odd that I don't like them in potato salad. Maybe it's because of my feeling that they are generally used as a stretcher in potato salad rather than as a flavorer.

4 cups cooked potatoes cut in
small cubes
2 cups finely chopped celery
¼ large sour pickle, finely
chopped

Mayonnaise
4 hard-boiled eggs (mash whole
egg with table fork)

A small quantity of minced pimiento adds an attractive color note.
Blend ingredients in order given, adding mayonnaise in quantity desired. (Unless homemade mayonnaise well seasoned with red pepper is used, cayenne pepper may be added.) Then add eggs blending in lightly or cut in quarters and garnish salad with these.

Snap Bean Salad

1 pound snaps (string beans)
½ cup boiling water

¼ cup Roquefort or blue cheese
dressing
½ teaspoon salt

String snaps, then slice diagonally in 1-inch pieces. Cook in saucepan,
covered, with boiling water and salt. Boil rapidly until snaps are
barely tender, about 10 minutes. Drain and chill. Serve on appropriate greens with Roquefort or blue cheese dressing made by
crumbling either variety of cheese in French dressing, using about
1 tablespoonful of cheese to ¼ cup of dressing.

Waldorf Salad Jelly

1 pint of prepared gelatin (1 envelope. Recipe is shown on brand I
use). Juice of 1 lemon. Just as gelatin starts to congeal, add 1 cup
of cubed, firm, tart apples (peeled), 1 cup diced celery, ½ cup
chopped walnuts, mixed well with salt and white pepper to taste
and paprika for looks. Pour into individual molds and refrigerate
until firm. Serve on salad greens with mayonnaise.

Water Cress Salad

3 tablespoons garlic vinegar
6 tablespoons olive oil
1 teaspoon dry mustard
½ teaspoon Worcestershire sauce

Garlic salt, pepper, and tabasco
(just a dash) to taste
2 teaspoons brown sugar
3 oz. Roquefort cheese

Add Roquefort cheese, crumbled, after mixing other ingredients. Add additional oil or vinegar if desired. Pour dressing over water cress in wooden bowl, sparingly. Toss well before serving.

Mayonnaise

2 egg yolks
1 pint salad oil
Juice of 1 lemon

¼ teaspoon salt
½ teaspoon red pepper

Beat egg yolks (preferably chilled, I think) with wire whisk and add oil (also chilled) very gingerly until there is a definite thickening of the mixture. Then add part of lemon juice, the salt, and red pepper. Continue beating and adding oil alternately with lemon juice. I like it very stiff and these proportions of the named ingredients will produce that result. If the mixture refuses to thicken as it sometimes does in the early stages, it spoils my satisfaction with the finished product, but the thickness can be retrieved by beating another egg yolk and adding mixture to it slowly, or 1 teaspoonful of hot water will sometimes start the thickening process again.

Boiled Salad Dressing

1 teaspoon salt
1 teaspoon dry mustard
¼ cup sugar
¼ teaspoon red pepper
1 teaspoon flour

2 tablespoons butter, melted
2 egg yolks
½ cup milk
½ cup apple cider vinegar

Mix dry ingredients; add egg yolks, slightly beaten, butter, milk, and vinegar (last two items slowly). Cook in double boiler about 10 minutes, or until of desired thickness. Avoid overcooking or it will curdle. In the event it does curdle, beat with rotary egg beater until smooth.

Salad Dressing (Uncooked)

1 pint homemade mayonnaise
2 hard-boiled eggs, finely
  chopped
½ cup apple cider vinegar
2 teaspoons prepared horseradish

2 teaspoons Worcestershire sauce
1 clove garlic, ground
Salt and pepper to taste
Dash of tabasco

Mix above ingredients together and place in screw-top jar until ready to use. Refrigerate. Makes about 1 quart.

SAUCES

Barbecue Sauce for Steak

⅔ cup strong black coffee
⅓ cup butter
2 teaspoonfuls Worcestershire
  sauce

1½ teaspoonfuls dry mustard
1 tablespoonful lemon juice
1 teaspoonful sugar
Dash of tabasco

Combine all ingredients in saucepan. Heat, stirring until butter melts. Brush over steak as it broils.

Brandy Sauce for Ham

Bring to a boil 1 quart apple cider or juice, 1 pound brown sugar, 6 cloves, and juice of 2 oranges. Remove from stove and add 2 ounces of brandy. Serve hot.

Cocktail Sauce

This is my preferred cocktail sauce.

1 cup tomato catsup
2 tablespoons lemon juice
½ teaspoon salt
1 tablespoon prepared horseradish

¼ teaspoon tabasco
1 teaspoon grated onion
(optional)

Mix ingredients thoroughly and refrigerate long enough to chill completely. Makes about 1¼ cups of sauce.

Cranberry Sauce

2 cups sugar
2 cups water

4 cups cranberries
Pinch of salt

Boil sugar, salt, and water gently for 5 minutes. Add cranberries, cover and simmer for 15 minutes at least (I like a very thick sauce that congeals under refrigeration), without stirring. Allow to cool without removing lid. Makes 1½ pints to 1 quart of sauce, depending on the consistency desired.

Cream Sauce

1 tablespoon butter
1 tablespoon flour
½ teaspoon salt
Few grains white pepper

Dash of tabasco
1 egg
1 cup milk

Melt butter in heavy saucepan; stir in flour and seasonings. Cook over low heat and stir until frothy all over, then draw to cooler part of stove and stir in beaten egg. Continue to stir while adding milk, hot or cold. Cook until thick, stirring until smooth. I think the addition of an egg adds so much in the way of flavor to sauce of this character, that this is my preferred recipe.

Creamed Chicken Sauce

2 tablespoons butter
2 tablespoons flour
½ teaspoon salt
1 cup chicken stock
1 cup milk

1 bay leaf, 6 peppercorns, 1 clove
1 small onion sliced, a few celery tops and a small sliced carrot
Dash of tabasco

Melt butter in saucepan; add flour and salt and blend until smooth. Stir in stock and milk (cold) gradually. Add other seasonings, and cook over direct heat, stirring constantly until sauce boils and becomes thick and smooth. Strain.

Fruit Fritter Sauce (for Fruit Fritters served as dessert)

½ cup currant jelly
2 tablespoons hot water
2 teaspoons lemon juice
Dash of salt

Dash of nutmeg
2 tablespoons chopped raisins
3 Maraschino cherries, chopped
1 teaspoon cherry juice

Combine and blend well jelly, hot water, lemon juice, salt, and nutmeg. Stir in raisins, cherries, and cherry juice. Serve with hot fruit fritters.

Hollandaise Sauce

2 egg yolks
½ teaspoon salt
Dash of tabasco

½ cup butter, melted
1 tablespoon lemon juice

Beat egg yolks until light. Add salt and tabasco. Place this mixture in top of double boiler over hot water, or in heavy crockery bowl set in pan of hot water (do not let water boil). Add 3 tablespoons melted butter a little at a time, beating constantly. Beat in rest of butter alternately with lemon juice. Cook until thick or about 10 minutes. If sauce separates, water was too hot or sauce cooked too rapidly.

Stir in a little boiling water drop by drop, beating constantly. If necessary to reheat, use top of double boiler over warm not hot water.

Hollandaise Sauce (newer method)

¼ pound butter, melted
3 egg yolks
1 tablespoon lemon juice

⅛ teaspoon salt
Dash of tabasco
3 tablespoons boiling water

To melted butter add egg yolks one at a time, beating well between each addition. Add lemon juice, salt, and tabasco. Heat water in bottom of double boiler (do not allow to boil). Put mixture into top and add 3 tablespoons boiling water. Cook 10 minutes, stirring constantly. Keep upper pan ¼ inch from water in lower pan and allow the steam to do the cooking. If feasible, rest upper pan on something but never allow upper pan to touch water in bottom pan.

Horseradish Sauce

½ pint heavy cream
1 cup applesauce

¼ cup prepared horseradish

Whip cream. Fold in applesauce and horseradish. Ready to serve when thoroughly mixed. Delicious accompaniment for ham.

Tomato Sauce

1 tablespoon minced onion
4 tablespoons butter
4 tablespoons flour
¼ teaspoon salt
⅛ teaspoon pepper

1 tablespoon Worcestershire
  sauce
Dash of tabasco
2 cups tomato juice

Sauté onions in butter until soft. Add flour, salt, pepper, Worcestershire sauce and tabasco. Blend well. Stir in tomato juice. Cook until thickened, stirring constantly.

White Sauce (Thin) (for Medium, use double, for Thick, use triple amount of butter and flour)

1 tablespoon butter
1 tablespoon flour
½ teaspoon salt

1 cup milk
Dash of tabasco

Melt butter in pan; add flour and salt and blend until smooth. Stir in cold milk gradually and cook over direct heat, stirring constantly until sauce boils and becomes thick and smooth. Remove from heat. Add tabasco. Should there be lumps, they can usually be removed by beating with a rotary beater. Makes about 1 cup. If necessary may be kept for several hours in double boiler over warm water, stirring occasionally, until ready for use.

Wine Sauce

2 cups sugar
4 tablespoons butter
1 cup boiling water
2 eggs, separated

Dash of nutmeg
1 cup of wine (dry red, dry white
    or Burgundy)

Beat sugar and butter together thoroughly. Add boiling water and put in double boiler over moderate heat. When mixture simmers, add yolks of eggs, well beaten, and the nutmeg. Stir until mixture thickens, then add stiffly beaten egg whites and wine.

Cakes and Cookies (and Cake Frostings)

Angel Food Cake

1 cup plus 2 tablespoons sifted
    cake flour (or 1 cup unbleached
    bread flour and 2 tablespoons
    arrowroot or cornstarch)
1½ cup sifted granulated sugar

1¼ cups (10 to 12) egg whites
¼ teaspoon salt
1¼ teaspoons cream of tartar
1 teaspoon vanilla
¼ teaspoon almond extract

Sift flour once, measure, add ½ cup sugar and sift together 4 times.
Beat egg whites and salt with wire whisk until foamy. Sprinkle in

cream of tartar and beat until eggs are stiff enough to hold up in soft peaks. Add remaining cup of sugar by sprinkling four tablespoonfuls at a time over egg whites and beating until well blended. Add flavorings and beat again to blend well. Add flour and sugar mixture in four additions, sifting it over the egg whites. Fold in each addition with flat wire whisk. When well blended, pour mixture into ungreased tube pan, about 10 inches in diameter. Bake in 375-degree oven for 30 to 35 minutes, or until cake is delicately browned and springs back when lightly pressed with finger tip. Remove from oven and invert pan in such a way that cake does not rest on upper crust. If pan has no supports to permit this, put knife handle or fork under two sides. Leave inverted until cake has cooled thoroughly. Then loosen cake around sides and at tube with thin-bladed knife and remove from pan. Serve as is or cover with any favorite white frosting, whipped cream, or top cake slices with fruited whipped cream.

In the interest of good health I usually use 1 cup of an unbleached flour plus 2 tablespoonfuls of arrowroot which produces a lovely cake.

Burnt-Almond Cake

½ cup butter
1 cup sugar
3 egg whites, unbeaten
½ teaspoon almond extract

2 cups cake flour, sifted
3 teaspoons baking powder
¼ teaspoon salt
⅔ cup milk

Cream butter and sugar. Add unbeaten egg whites, one at a time, beating well after each addition. Add almond extract. Sift flour, baking powder, and salt together. Add alternately with milk to first mixture beating until well blended. Bake in two greased 9-inch layer-cake pans in 375-degree oven, 25 to 30 minutes. Cool on cake racks.

(*Frosting*)
1 cup butter
2⅔ cup XXXX sugar
Hot milk or cream

½ teaspoon almond extract
1½ cups blanched almonds

2 tablespoons salad oil

Cream butter. Add sugar gradually, with sufficient hot milk or cream to make it of good spreading consistency. Add almond extract. Put cake layers together with frosting. Frost top and sides.

Put almonds in shallow pan with about 2 tablespoons salad oil. Place in 450-degree oven. Sitr often until almonds are deep golden brown. Drain on absorbent paper. Crush almonds quite fine with rolling pin. Cover entire cake with almonds, pressing lightly into frosting.

Burnt-Sugar Cake

2 cups cake flour
2 teaspoons baking powder
1/4 teaspoon soda
1/4 teaspoon salt
1/2 cup butter
1 cup sugar

1 egg, slightly beaten
1 egg yolk slightly beaten
1 cup cold water
1 1/2 tablespoons burnt sugar
   syrup

Sift flour, baking powder, soda, and salt together. Cream butter, and add sugar gradually. Add egg and egg yolk and beat until smooth and light. Add water alternately with sifted dry ingredients. Add burnt-sugar syrup. (To make burnt-sugar syrup, heat 1/4 cup sugar in heavy skillet. When melted, add 1/4 cup hot water and stir until dissolved. Cool.) Pour into two 9-inch layer-cake pans and bake in 350-degree oven for 30 to 35 minutes.

Burnt-Sugar Frosting

2 egg whites
1 1/2 cups sugar
Pinch of salt
1/3 cup water

2 teaspoons dark corn syrup
2 tablespoons burnt-sugar syrup
Pecan meats

With rotary beater, beat together in double boiler (over boiling water) egg whites, sugar, salt, water, and corn syrup. Beat about 10 minutes, or until frosting thickens and holds its shape. Remove from over boiling water, add burnt-sugar syrup, and continue beating until stiff enough to spread. Decorate with pecan meats.

Caramel Cake

½ cup butter
2 cups light brown sugar
4 eggs, separated
1½ cups sifted cake flour
1½ teaspoons baking powder

¼ cup milk
2 teaspoonfuls vanilla
1 cup chopped nut meats
(optional)
½ teaspoonful salt

Cream butter and sugar together. Beat in egg yolks, one at a time. Sift together flour and baking powder and beat into butter mixture alternately with milk. Add vanilla and nut meats (if used). Add salt to egg whites and beat until stiff. Fold gently into cake batter. Bake in two greased 9-inch layer-cake pans in 375-degree oven for about 20 minutes. Remove layers from pans and cool on cake racks. Frost with:

Caramel Nut Frosting

2 cups light brown sugar
1 cup light cream
3 tablespoonfuls butter

¼ cup chopped nut meats
1 teaspoonful vanilla

Combine sugar and cream. Stir until sugar is dissolved and boil mixture without stirring to soft ball stage. Add butter. Remove frosting from heat and cool. Then add vanilla and beat until thick and creamy. Stir in nut meats. If frosting is too stiff to spread, add a small amount of cream.

Cheese Cake, Martha's

(*Crust*)

1 cup flour, sifted
¼ cup sugar
1 teaspoon grated lemon rind
Pulp from small piece of vanilla
bean (or 1 teaspoon vanilla
extract)

1 egg yolk
½ cup butter
Pinch of salt

Blend flour, sugar, lemon rind, and vanilla bean (or extract). Make a well in the center and add egg yolk, butter and pinch of salt. Mix with hands until well blended, adding a small amount of cold water if necessary to make a light dough. Wrap dough in wax paper and chill for one hour.

Roll out chilled dough until only ⅛ inch thick and place it over oiled *bottom* of a 9-inch spring-form cake pan. Remove the excess dough by pressing it against edge of pan with fingers. Bake circle of dough in a hot oven (400 degrees) for about 15 minutes or until it is a light brown in color. When it has cooled, butter the sides of the spring-form pan and place it over the base. Roll out remaining dough to ⅛ inch thick and cut a band to fit the sides. Line the sides of the pan with this band of dough, pressing it firmly against the bottom crust. Fill the prepared pan with cheese filling (see below) and bake in a very hot oven (550 degrees) for 10 minutes. Reduce oven temperature to very slow (200 degrees) and continue baking for one hour. Cool cheese cake before cutting it.

A much easier crust to make but not so good as the one above is the following:

1 box zwieback	⅔ cup soft butter
½ cup sugar	

Roll zwieback into fine crumbs. Mix crumbs with sugar and butter. Line bottom and sides of spring-form pan with mixture and chill in refrigerator overnight to insure a firm crust.

(Filling)

1 cup sugar	1 teaspoonful vanilla
1 tablespoon flour	1 teaspoonful lemon juice
18 ounces cream cheese	Grated rind of half a lemon
6 eggs, separated	1 cup heavy cream, whipped

Cream together sugar, flour, and cream cheese. Stir in well-beaten egg yolks, vanilla, lemon juice, and grated lemon rind. Stir in whipped cream. Fold in stiffly beaten egg whites. Pour mixture into prepared pan (using either crust of zwieback or see crust recipe above) and bake in moderate (350-degree) oven for one hour. Turn off the oven, open the door and let cake cool in oven for one hour.

Cocoanut Cake

½ cup butter
1½ cups sugar
3 eggs, separated
3 cups cake flour
½ teaspoon salt

3 teaspoons baking powder
1 cup cocoanut milk or 1 cup
milk
1 teaspoon vanilla

Cream butter and ¾ cup sugar. Beat 3 egg yolks until light; add to this the other ¾ cup of sugar. Beat well and add to first mixture of butter and sugar. Sift, then measure flour to which add salt and baking powder, sifting mixture 3 times. Scald milk and beat alternately with flour into butter and sugar. Add vanilla and beat thoroughly. Then fold in lightly egg whites stiffly beaten. Bake in two 9-inch layer-cake pans in 375-degree oven for about 20 minutes. Turn out on cake racks and let cool before frosting with Cocoanut Frosting:

1¾ cups sugar
⅔ cup water
Pinch of salt
2 egg whites

1 teaspoon vanilla
1 or 2 cups freshly grated
cocoanut

Boil sugar and water together until it forms soft ball in cool water. Add salt to egg whites and beat until stiff; gradually pour syrup into eggs, beating all the time. Add vanilla. Mix ⅔ of cocoanut in the frosting and spread between layers and on outside of cake. Sprinkle balance of cocoanut over top and sides of cake after frosting.

Dark Fruit Cake

1 pound seeded raisins
1 pound seedless raisins
1 pound currants
½ pound dates
½ pound citron
¼ pound orange peel
¼ pound lemon peel

¼ pound almonds, shelled
¼ pound English walnuts,
shelled
¼ pound candied cherries
¼ pound candied pineapple
4 ounces currant jelly
1 cup peach or apple brandy

The day before the cake is baked, cut pineapple in small pieces; cut cherries and dates in quarters, citron and other peels in narrow strips. Blanch almonds and cut in slivers. Add almonds and walnut meats, raisins, and currants to prepared fruit. Mix with jelly. Over this mixture pour the cup of peach or apple brandy and store overnight in a cool place. The next day, make cake out of the following added to fruit and nut mixture above:

½ pound butter	½ teaspoon nutmeg
1 pound sugar	½ teaspoon cloves
6 eggs, separated	½ teaspoon mace
2 cups cake flour	½ teaspoon salt
1 teaspoon allspice	½ cup sherry
1 teaspoon cinnamon	

Cream butter with half of the sugar. Add well-beaten egg yolks to which has been added the rest of the sugar. Blend well. Add stiffly beaten egg whites and mix with the fruit. Sift flour with dry seasonings and add to the batter and follow with the sherry. Use additional flour if needed to make a stiff batter. Line a tube cake pan, preferably iron, with wax paper or foil wrap. Foil wrap is preferable if the mold has a design. Grease and fill with batter to within 1½ inches of the top. If you like steamed fruit cakes, steam for about 3 hours; then bake in 350-degree oven about 30 minutes. Otherwise, bake cake about 3½ hours in a 350-degree oven. If the cake is to be kept for some time, moisten occasionally with sherry.

Devil's Food Cake

2 cups cake flour	½ cup sour milk
1 teaspoon baking powder	1 teaspoon vanilla
1 cup butter	½ cup boiling water
¾ cup sugar	6 squares unsweetened choco-
2 cups light brown sugar, sifted	late, melted
3 egg yolks, unbeaten	1¼ teaspoons soda
3 whole eggs, unbeaten	

Sift flour once, add baking powder and sift again. Cream butter thoroughly; add sugar gradually, and cream together until light and fluffy. Add egg yolks; beat thoroughly. Add eggs, one at a time, beating vigorously after the addition of each egg. Add flour alternately with milk, a small amount at a time. Beat after each addition until smooth. Add vanilla. Add boiling water to chocolate and mix well. Cool, add soda. Combine chocolate mixture and cake batter and beat vigorously for three minutes. Pour into two greased pans (8 x 8 x 2"), filling each pan two-thirds full. Bake in 350-degree oven 1 hour. Frost between layers and top and sides of cake with Divinity Frosting (p. 131).

White Fruit Cake

½ pound butter	½ pound citron
1 pound sugar	1 pound white raisins
4 eggs, separated	4 cups flour, sifted
1 pound blanched almonds	Pinch of salt
¼ pound candied cherries	½ cup sherry
¼ pound candied pineapple	½ pound fresh cocoanut, grated

Cream butter and sugar together. Add well-beaten egg yolks. Cut blanched almonds into narrow strips and the fruits into small pieces. Dredge fruit in part of the flour sifted with the salt. Add rest of the flour and sherry alternately to butter and sugar mixture. Stir in cocoanut and floured fruits. Fold in stiffly beaten egg whites. Bake in 250- to 300-degree oven about 4 hours.

For extra luxury in fruit cakes, use the following frosting:

1½ cups XXXX sugar, sifted	1 tablespoon hot milk or coffee
2 tablespoons butter, melted	cream
1 teaspoon vanilla	

Beat sugar and melted butter together vigorously. Add vanilla and 1 tablespoon more or less of milk or cream to make frosting of good spreading consistency. If desired, a topping of almond paste may be put on under the frosting as follows: Put 1 cup of blanched almonds through fine nut grinder of food chopper. Combine the ground almonds with 1 cup sifted XXXX sugar and 1 unbeaten egg white. If desired use 1 or 2 drops of almond extract for additional flavoring. Spread on cake after cake is cold. I love pleasant superstitions, such as the one that as many different kinds of fruit cake as you eat on New Year's Day, that many pieces of good luck will you have during the year.

Lane Cake

Like most well-known recipes there are several versions of this lovely cake, some of which call for cocoanut, and for brandy in place of bourbon.

(Cake Batter)

1 cup butter	2 teaspoons baking powder
2 cups sugar	Pinch of salt
1 cup milk	8 egg whites, stiffly beaten
4 cups cake flour	1 teaspoon vanilla

Cream butter well, add sugar; then add milk alternately with dry ingredients which have been sifted together. Fold in egg whites and lastly vanilla. Bake in three 8-inch round layer-cake pans.

(Filling)

8 egg yolks	1 cup white raisins
1 cup sugar	1 cup shelled pecans
¼ pound butter, softened	½ cup bourbon

Beat egg yolks until light. Add sugar, butter, raisins, and pecans. Stir all together and cook until thick in double boiler. Just before spreading, add bourbon. Spread between layers. Frost top and sides with favorite white icing.

Robert E. Lee Cake

10 eggs, separated	Grated peel 1 lemon
2 cups sugar	2 cups cake flour
1 teaspoon lemon juice	¼ teaspoon salt
1 teaspoon orange juice	

Beat egg yolks until lemon-colored. Add sugar, fruit juices, and lemon peel. Fold in stiffly beaten egg whites. Then add flour sifted with salt. Bake in four 8-inch ungreased round layer-cake pans.

(*Frosting*)

3 cups sugar
1 cup water
3 egg whites, stiffly beaten
1 tablespoon lemon juice

Grated peel 1 orange
Grated peel 1 lemon
1 cup grated fresh cocoanut

Boil sugar and water together until it forms a soft ball in cool water. Pour over egg whites beating constantly. Add lemon juice and grated orange and lemon peel to frosting. Spread between layers and on top and sides of cake. Sprinkle cocoanut all over outside of cake. This famous cake has several variants.

Nut Cake

4 eggs, separated
1 cup sugar
½ cup potato flour

1 teaspoon baking powder
1 teaspoon vanilla

Beat egg yolks until light. Add sugar, then flour sifted with baking powder. Fold in stiffly beaten egg whites lightly. Blend in vanilla. Bake in shallow pan in 375-degree oven for 15 or 20 minutes.

(*Frosting*)

½ cup butter
1 pound XXXX sugar
1 teaspoon vanilla
Coffee cream

1 pound salted peanuts, ground in fine grinder of food chopper

Cream butter and add sugar. Beat until well blended. Add vanilla. Add small amount of cream if too stiff for spreading. Cut cake in square serving portions; frost and roll in peanuts.

Nut and Fruit Cake

4 eggs, separated
1 cup candied cherries
8 ounces pitted dates
1 cup Brazil nut meats
1 cup black walnut meats
1 cup English walnut meats

1 cup pecan meats
1 cup almond meats, blanched
1 cup sugar
1 cup cake flour, sifted
Pinch of salt
2 tablespoons vanilla

Beat yolks and whites separately, then combine. Add fruit, nuts, sugar, flour, and salt which have been previously well blended. Add vanilla. Bake about 2½ hours in a 300-degree oven, preferably in an [iron] tube mold such as is usually used for fruit cake.

Pound Cake

4 cups cake flour (sifted 3 times for lightness)
1 pound butter (use only ¾ pound if country butter is used)

1 dozen eggs, separated
1 pound sugar
Pinch of salt
1 tablespoon brandy
1 tablespoon lemon juice

Cream flour and butter together until light. Beat egg yolks, sugar, and salt together until light and all sugar grains are dissolved. Mix the whole together, beating vigorously. Add stiffly beaten egg whites, folding in completely. Add brandy and lemon juice, blending in lightly. Bake in [iron] tube mold for 1½ hours in oven preheated to 350 degrees.

Rocky Mountain Cake

1¼ pounds butter
1½ cups sugar
3 eggs, separated
1 teaspoon soda
1 cup buttermilk

2 cups cake flour
½ teaspoon salt
1 teaspoon cream of tartar
1 teaspoon vanilla extract
1 teaspoon lemon extract

Cream butter and sugar together. Beat egg yolks until thick and light-colored. Beat whites until stiff. Dissolve soda in buttermilk. Beat egg yolks into butter and sugar mixture. Sift flour with salt and cream of tartar, and add alternately with buttermilk to butter, sugar, and egg-yolk mixture. Add flavoring extracts. Fold in egg whites last. Bake in three 8-inch greased round layer-cake pans in 350-degree oven about 20 minutes.

(*Frosting*)

3 cups sugar
1 cup water
3 tablespoons light corn syrup

3 egg whites
Pinch of salt

Instead of water, use milk from a fresh cocoanut if available. Boil sugar, corn syrup, and water together to hard-ball stage. Then pour syrup slowly onto the beaten whites of 3 eggs with salt, beating constantly. Beat thoroughly and while still warm, add the following:

⅛ ounce pitted dates
⅛ ounce figs
4 ounces sliced citron
Grated meat of 1 large cocoanut
   (reserve ⅓ of cocoanut for
   outside of cake.)
4 ounces candied orange peel

4 ounces candied lemon peel
4 ounces candied red cherries
4 ounces candied green cherries
1 12-ounce package raisins
4 ounces candied red pineapple
4 ounces candied green pineapple
1 cup finely chopped nut meats

Frost between layers and on outside of cake generously with frosting. Sprinkle cocoanut on top and sides of cake.

This is a fruit cake with fruits and nut meats in frosting instead of in batter. Rocky Mountain Cake is said to take its name from the fact that folks long ago used to decorate this cake with bits of rock candy. The original recipe apparently called for such decoration.

Rum Cake

1 cup butter
2 cups sugar
1 cup milk
3½ cups cake flour

8 egg whites
3½ teaspoons baking powder
1 teaspoon vanilla
Pinch of salt

Cream butter and sugar together until light. Add ⅓ each of milk, flour, and stiffly beaten egg whites at a time, beating for 2 minutes after each addition. Keep out 2 tablespoons flour and mix baking powder with it. Add this mixture after the preliminary beating. Then beat for 5 minutes. Add vanilla and salt last. Bake in four 8-inch greased cake pans for 20 to 30 minutes in 350-degree oven. Turn out on racks and cool before adding filling.

(Filling)

2½ cups XXXX sugar
1 cup butter

½ cup rum

Cream sugar and butter together until light and smooth. Add rum and beat in well. Refrigerate until firm enough to spread. After spreading filling between cake layers, return cake to refrigerator until filling is firm.

(Frosting)

2 cups sugar
¼ cup (about) water
2 egg whites

12 marshmallows
1 to 2 teaspoons rum

Dissolve sugar in water. Boil together until syrup will form soft ball in cool water. Pour slowly over stiffly beaten egg whites, beating constantly. While mixture is hot, add marshmallows, a few at a time, and the rum. Spread over top and sides of cake. Refrigerate until ready to use.

Tipsy Cake

1 cup sugar
5 eggs, separated
1 teaspoon vinegar
1 teaspoon vanilla
1 cup flour
¼ teaspoon salt

Blanched almonds
1 quart boiled custard
8 tablespoons sherry
Whipped cream
Maraschino cherries

Beat sugar and egg whites together until meringue is stiff. Fold in egg yolks well beaten. Add vinegar and vanilla. Stir in flour and salt sifted together. Bake in oblong pan in 300-degree oven for about 1 hour. Turn out on rack and, when cool, cut in half. Decorate edges of top half with quartered blanched almonds. To the custard (chilled), add sherry. Cover bottom half of cake with this mixture. Top with decorated half of cake and spread custard mixture over sides. Reserve rest of custard mixture to serve with cake at the table. In addition to almonds, frost cake top with whipped cream and garnish with Maraschino cherries. Chill 12 hours before serving.

White Layer Cake

2½ cups cake flour
3 teaspoons baking powder
¼ teaspoon cream of tartar
½ cup butter

1½ cups sifted sugar
½ cup milk
1 teaspoon vanilla
6 egg whites, stiffly beaten

Sift flour once, measure, add baking powder and cream of tartar and sift together 3 times. Cream butter thoroughly, add sugar gradually, and cream together until light and fluffy. Add flour, alternately with milk, a small amount at a time. Beat after each addition until smooth. Add vanilla; fold in egg whites. Bake in two greased 9-inch cake pans in a 375-degree oven about 30 minutes. Frost with favorite frosting between layers and on top and sides.

Southern Belle Cake

2¼ cups cake flour
3 teaspoons baking powder
½ teaspoon salt
1 teaspoon mace
1 cup butter
1½ cups sugar

4 eggs, separated
⅔ cup orange juice
Rind of 1 orange
Whipped cream, sweetened
Grated orange peel

Sift flour, baking powder, salt and ½ teaspoon mace together three times. Cream butter and sugar together well; add well-beaten egg yolks to butter-sugar mixture. Next add dry ingredients, orange juice, and grated rind and beat well. Then fold in stiffly beaten whites. Bake in three greased 8-inch pans in 350-degree oven about 30 minutes. Allow to cool and then spread orange filling between and on top of cake and cover with sweetened whipped cream into which ½ teaspoon mace has been blended. Sprinkle with grated orange peel.

(Orange Filling)

½ cup sugar
2 tablespoons flour
Pinch of salt
4 tablespoons orange juice

½ teaspoon lemon juice
2 tablespoons grated orange rind
1 egg
1 tablespoon butter

Sift sugar, flour, and salt together. Add orange and lemon juice and orange rind. Add slightly beaten egg and butter. Mix well in top of double boiler and cook until thick and smooth (about 10 minutes), stirring frequently. Cool partially before frosting cake.

CAKE FROSTINGS (COOKED)

Divinity Frosting

3 cups sugar
1 teaspoon light corn syrup
1⅓ cups boiling water

4 egg whites
Pinch of salt
1 teaspoon vanilla

Combine sugar, corn syrup, and water. Place in saucepan over low flame, stirring constantly until sugar is dissolved and mixture boils. Continue to cook until a small amount of syrup forms a soft ball in cool water. Then pour in a fine stream over stiffly beaten egg whites and salt, beating constantly. Add vanilla and continue beating until stiff enough to spread on cake.

Egg Yolk Frosting

2 cups sugar
1 cup hot water
1 teaspoon light corn syrup
4 egg yolks

Pinch of salt
¼ teaspoon cream of tartar
1 teaspoon lemon extract

Boil sugar, water, and syrup together until it forms a soft ball in cool water; set aside in a warm place. Beat egg yolks and salt until light and lemon-colored. Pour syrup over yolks in thin stream, beating constantly. Add cream of tartar and lemon extract and continue beating until right consistency for spreading.

Lemon Frosting

2 cups sugar
4 eggs
4 tablespoons butter

Juice of 4 lemons
Grated rind of 2 lemons
Pinch of salt

Beat all together and cook in double boiler until of the consistency of jelly. This will be sufficient for 4 cake layers.

7-minute Frosting

2 egg whites
¾ cup sugar
2½ tablespoons cold water

½ teaspoon cream of tartar
Pinch of salt
1 teaspoon lemon extract

Put unbeaten egg whites, sugar, cold water, cream of tartar, and salt, in top part of double boiler. Beat (preferably with rotary beater) until well blended. Place top of double boiler over hard-boiling water in bottom part and beat continuously for 7 minutes. At that time the mixture should stand up in peaks. Remove from fire and cool. When cool and stiff enough to use as a frosting, add lemon extract. Spread on cake with spatula or table knife.

CAKE FROSTINGS (UNCOOKED)

Butter Frosting

4 tablespoons salted butter
2½ cups XXXX sugar
Pinch of salt

1 teaspoon vanilla
1 tablespoon cream

Cream butter well. Add 1 cup of sugar, pinch of salt, and vanilla. Add alternately remaining sugar and cream.

Chocolate Frosting

2 squares chocolate, melted
1 pound XXXX sugar
Pinch of salt
2 tablespoons butter, milk or

cream, to make frosting the
right consistency for spreading
1 teaspoon vanilla

Blend melted chocolate, sugar, and salt thoroughly. Add butter, milk or cream until frosting is of desired consistency, then add vanilla. Beat well.

Lemon Frosting

Grated rind of 2 lemons
4 tablespoons soft butter
2 egg yolks, unbeaten

4 cups XXXX sugar (sifted)
Juice of 2 lemons (about)
Pinch of salt

Cream together lemon rind and butter. Add egg yolks and mix well. Add sugar alternately with lemon juice until of the right consistency to spread. Beat (not stir) until smooth. Add salt.
This makes sufficient for two 9-inch layers. A little more or less lemon juice may be used according to the size of the lemons, to make frosting of good spreading consistency. Beating will make it stiffen up better than a stirred frosting, and it will harden to a pretty glaze on top and be soft underneath. For orange frosting, use rind of an orange instead of 1 of the lemons, and half and half lemon and orange juice.

Water Frosting

1 pound XXXX sugar
Pinch of salt

Boiling water
Flavoring

Pour sufficient boiling water over sugar and pinch of salt to make a thick frosting, and add any flavoring desired. Then spread on cake. This frosting is quickly made and hardens at once.

COOKIES
Brown Sugar Cookies

1 cup butter
2 cups light brown sugar
2 eggs
½ teaspoonful salt

1 teaspoonful soda
3½ cups flour
1 cup nut meats
1 teaspoonful vanilla

Cream butter and sugar together; add well-beaten eggs. Sift salt and soda with flour and add to butter mixture. Add finely chopped nuts and vanilla. Shape into long roll and refrigerate overnight. Slice off in thin slices. Bake in 325-degree oven for about 10 minutes on greased cooky sheet.

Cocoanut Dream Bars

½ cup butter
½ cup light brown sugar

Pinch of salt
1 cup flour, sifted

Cream butter, sugar, and salt together until fluffy. Add flour. Pack into a greased pan (round 8-inch cake pan or 8 x 8 x 2″ pan) and bake in 350-degree oven 10 minutes. Remove from oven and top with:

2 eggs
1 cup light brown sugar
3 tablespoonfuls flour, sifted
Pinch of salt

1½ cups fresh grated cocoanut
1 cup nut meats
1 teaspoonful vanilla

Beat eggs and other ingredients together. Spread on top of first mixture. Return to oven and bake until brown and firm. Cool before cutting into servings as desired.

Hazlenut Cookies

1 pound hazelnuts, shelled and
   ground (nut-butter grinder)
½ pound XXXX sugar
2 eggs
1 cup flour, sifted

¼ teaspoonful baking powder
Pinch of salt
1 tablespoonful cream
1 teaspoonful vanilla

Combine hazelnuts ground into a butter with sugar. Add well-beaten eggs. Sift flour, baking powder and salt together and add to hazelnut mixture. Add cream and vanilla. Add extra flour if necessary to get dough stiff enough to roll out on floured board. Cut into desired shape and size and place on lightly floured cooky sheet. Bake in 300-degree oven for 10 minutes. Do not brown. Tops of cookies will puff up, then deflate. When cool, remove from cooky sheet with spatula and sprinkle lightly with sifted XXXX sugar. Stored in tightly covered tin, cookies will mellow and improve with age.

Orange Crisps

½ cup butter
1 cup sugar
1 egg
Grated rind of 1 lemon and 1
   orange

3 tablespoons orange juice
   (I usually use half lemon
   and half orange juice)
3 cups flour
½ teaspoon baking powder
¼ teaspoon soda
¼ teaspoon salt

Cream butter and sugar together; Add well-beaten egg. Blend well. Add grated rind and fruit juice. Sift flour, baking powder, soda, and salt together. Add to butter mixture. Mix thoroughly. Shape into long roll and chill until firm, preferably overnight. Slice off in thin slices and bake on greased baking sheet in 325-degree oven for 10 or 15 minutes.

Shortbread Cookies

1 cup butter   2 cups flour, sifted
1 cup XXXX sugar   Pinch of salt

Cream butter; add sugar gradually. Cream thoroughly. Stir in flour sifted with salt. Roll dough ¼ inch thick on floured board. Cut with cooky cutter. Bake on greased cooky sheet in 300-degree oven for about 25 minutes. Cookies should be dry but still light in color. Do not remove from cooky sheet until thoroughly cooled. Makes from 3 to 4 dozen cookies.

Desserts

Cashew Dessert

5 egg whites
Pinch of salt
1½ cups sugar

1½ cups ground cashew nuts
   (grind with fine nut grinder)
1 teaspoon vanilla

Beat egg whites stiff with salt. Add sugar. Fold in nuts. Blend in vanilla. Bake in four 8-inch cake pans, spreading batter thinly on bottom of pans. Bake in 300-degree oven until brown and crisp.

(Filling)

5 egg yolks
Pinch of salt
1½ cups sugar

½ cup water
1½ cups butter, creamed
4 tablespoons strong coffee

Beat egg yolks and salt together until thick. Cook sugar and water together until the syrup forms a soft ball in cup of cold water. Pour

137

egg yolks onto syrup gradually, beating constantly. Cool. Add butter and coffee. Beat thoroughly. Spread between layers and on outside. Refrigerate until serving time.

Crême Brulée

3 cups whipping cream, not
   whipped
6 egg yolks

Light brown sugar
Chopped, sweetened peaches

Heat cream to scalding in double boiler. Beat egg yolks until thick. Pour hot cream slowly over egg yolks and blend well. Return to fire and cook until thick, about 10 minutes, stirring constantly. Pour into baking dish and chill thoroughly. About 1 hour before serving, sprinkle the surface of the cream with a thin layer of light brown sugar, sifted. Place in 350-degree oven and broil until sugar is melted into a glaze on top of the custard. Cool. Spoon cream over sweetened chopped peaches in individual serving dishes.

Lemon Butter

1 pound sugar
3 lemons (juice and grated rind)

3 eggs

Blend sugar, grated rind, and lemon juice. Then beat in eggs, one at a time, beating thoroughly after each addition. Refrigerate and use as wanted on hot biscuits or over ice cream.

Dulcet Cream

Pears
Water
Sugar

Sherry
Nutmeg

Pare and core firm pears and cut into halves. Cover with water to which sugar has been added in the proportion desired. Simmer until tender. When cooked, remove pears. Add an equal amount of sherry to the syrup and pour it over the pears. Chill, then sprinkle nutmeg over them and serve with Dulcet Cream made as follows:

12 blanched almonds

½ cup milk

3 egg yolks

¾ cup heavy cream

¼ cup sherry

Almond extract

Chop or grind 12 blanched almonds and add them to ½ cup milk. Beat 3 egg yolks with ¾ cup heavy cream and ¼ cup sherry and add to almond-milk mixture. Cook in double boiler, stirring constantly until thickened and smooth. Add almond extract to suit the taste.

Fried Cream, Flambé

This dish is said to date back to the time of Queen Anne.

1 pint heavy cream

1 teaspoon Jamaica rum

⅛ teaspoon salt

¼ cup sugar

½ inch of stick cinnamon

3 tablespoons cornstarch (moistened in 3 tablespoons milk)

3 egg yolks

Crushed salted crackers

1 beaten egg, to which 2 tablespoons of water have been added

Ground almonds

Rum

Scald cream and add rum, salt, sugar, cinnamon, cornstarch, and egg yolks. Cook over hot water, stirring constantly, until the cream is thick and smooth and there's no taste of cornstarch. Pour it about ¾ of an inch thick into a flat dish (8 x 8 x 2″). Refrigerate until thoroughly chilled. Cut into squares or oblongs, roll in very finely crushed salted crackers, dip in beaten egg yolks and then in ground almonds, and fry in deep fat at 400 degrees, just long enough to brown the almonds. Pour on heated rum, set alight and serve flaming.

Boiled Custard

1 quart milk

6 egg yolks

½ cup sugar

Pinch of Salt

2 teaspoons vanilla

Put milk on stove in double boiler. Beat egg yolks, sugar, and salt together well. When milk is hot, but not boiling, stir half of it into the egg yolks and sugar mixture. Then stir this into milk still on stove. Cook until of desired thickness, about 10 minutes. Remove from heat and add vanilla. If custard curdles, beat with rotary egg beater until smooth.

Gingerbread (*Washington-Lewis family recipe revised*)

½ cup butter
½ cup light brown sugar
1 cup seeded raisins (optional)
1 cup dark molasses
½ cup warm milk
2 tablespoons ground ginger
1 teaspoon ground cinnamon
1 teaspoon ground mace

1 teaspoon ground nutmeg
1 wineglass (4 ounces) brandy
3 eggs
3 cups flour
1 teaspoon cream of tartar
1 orange (juice and grated rind)
1 teaspoon soda
¼ cup warm water

Cream butter and sugar together. Add raisins, molasses, milk, ginger, cinnamon, mace, and nutmeg. Add brandy. Beat eggs until light and add alternately with flour sifted with cream of tartar to sugar-butter mixture. Add juice and rind of orange. Dissolve soda in ¼ cup warm water and stir into batter. Beat for 5 minutes. Bake in two square (8 x 8 x 2″) or one long (14 x 8 x 3″) pan, well greased, in 350-degree oven about 1 hour.

Suggested toppings: put 1 cup brown sugar in a double boiler, add white of an egg and 2 tablespoons water. Beat over hot water for 7 minutes. Cool and spread on gingerbread.

Whip 1 cup cream stiff; add 1 teaspoon sugar, 3 drops vanilla and ¾ cup sweetened applesauce.

Gingerbread Sauce

3 tablespoons butter
1 cup XXXX sugar
2 eggs, separated

½ teaspoon vanilla
½ cup cream, whipped

Cream butter and sugar together. Add well-beaten egg yolks and beat for 5 minutes in top of double boiler over hot water. Remove from heat and fold in stiffly beaten egg whites, vanilla, and whipped cream.

As a substitute for whipping cream, especially in fruit desserts, add 1 thinly sliced banana to 1 egg white beaten until frothy, then whip to the consistency of whipped cream. Add 2 tablespoons of sugar and serve promptly.

Frosted Grapes

Wash and dry thoroughly any variety of grape. Dip into unbeaten egg white, coating each grape. Roll in granulated sugar. Place in refrigerator and allow to chill overnight or until sugar hardens. Mint leaves may be frosted by the same method.

Maids of Honor

This is an old English recipe well known to many Richmonders of an older day.

1 tablespoon strawberry, cherry
   or raspberry preserves
2 eggs
½ cup sugar
2 tablespoons flour, sifted

2 tablespoons butter, melted
½ cup ground almond meats
1 tablespoon sherry
Sprinkle of nutmeg

Line tart shells with rich pastry and spread on each 1 tablespoon of preserves. Beat eggs well, slowly adding sugar and flour which have been mixed together. Add butter and almonds, sherry and nutmeg. Spoon this filling on top of preserves in pastry shells and bake in 350-degree oven for about 30 minutes.

Meringue Shells

4 egg whites   1 cup sugar

Beat egg whites until foamy. Add sugar, a tablespoon at a time. Beat well after each addition. Then beat until stiff peaks form. Shape meringue shells on heavy brown paper (ungreased) on a cooky sheet. Hollow out centers with back of a teaspoon which has been dipped in warm water. Bake in 250-degree oven 60 to 75 minutes, or until dry. These quantities make 12 medium-size shells. Suggested fillings are frozen fruit mixtures, or sweetened crushed fruit.

Old English Trifle

10 Lady Fingers
10 Macaroons
Strawberry or raspberry jam
2 cups thick cold boiled custard
½ cup Madeira

2 ounces blanched and shredded almonds
1 tablespoon grated lemon peel
1 cup heavy cream
2 egg whites
¼ cup sugar

Cut lady fingers and macaroons in half and spread a layer of jam on each. Cover with other half. Lay a few in the bottom of a glass dish, alternating layers of lady fingers and macaroons. Moisten with Madeira, sprinkle with almonds and grated lemon peel and cover with cold custard. Over this put the cream whipped with egg whites and sugar. Decorate with cherries.

Oranges (Cooked)

6 oranges
½ cup light corn syrup

2 cups sugar
2 cups water

Boil oranges whole and unpeeled in water to cover for about 30 minutes, or until tender. Drain oranges and allow to cool. Boil together for 5 minutes, syrup, sugar, and water. Pour over cooked oranges which have been quartered and seeded. Cover and bake in 350-degree oven for about 1½ hours. Serve hot or cold for dessert, with crackers and cream cheese. May be kept for future use in sterile jars. Seal. This may also be used as an accompaniment for meat or poultry.

Peaches Celestial

6 large peaches
4 tablespoons candied ginger
   syrup
1 pint ice cream

Walnut meats, finely chopped
¼ cup candied ginger, finely
   chopped

Peel peaches and cut in halves. Remove stones. Put small quantity of ginger syrup (taken from candied ginger) on each half. Bake peaches in 350-degree oven until slightly brown. Cool. Fill centers with ice cream. Sprinkle walnut meats and ginger on top of ice cream.

Peach Cobbler

Peaches to fit your baking dish
1¼ cups sugar
⅓ cup butter

½ cup flour, sifted
Pinch of salt

Peel and halve peaches. Blend other ingredients together well and place over peaches in baking dish. Cook until surface of cobbler is golden brown and crisp in 350-degree oven.

Persimmon Pudding

2 cups persimmon pulp
3 eggs, well beaten
1¾ cups milk
2 cups flour
1 teaspoon soda
1 teaspoon salt

½ teaspoon ground cinnamon
½ teaspoon ground nutmeg
½ cup sugar
3 tablespoons melted butter
Cream, whipped or unwhipped

Mix persimmon pulp, eggs, and milk. Sift together flour, soda, salt, cinnamon, nutmeg, and sugar. Pour persimmon mixture into flour mixture and blend well. Add butter and beat again. Pour into 14 x 8 x 3″ buttered pan. Bake 1 hour in 300-degree oven. Chill, cut in squares and serve with cream.

Bing Cherry Ice Cream

2 cups light cream
½ cup sugar
¼ teaspoon salt
3 egg yolks
1½ cups heavy cream

1 cup drained Bing cherry
  halves
½ cup toasted slivered almonds
1¼ teaspoons almond extract
2½ tablespoons rum

Scald light cream over boiling water, then stir in sugar and salt. Beat egg yolks slightly in bowl and stir in a little of the hot cream mixture slowly, to prevent curdling. Stir this egg yolk mixture into the rest of the hot cream mixture and cook again over boiling water until the resulting soft custard coats the spoon. Stir constantly. Cool and add heavy cream, stiffly whipped. Turn into refrigerator tray and freeze partially, then stir in cherries, almonds, almond extract, and rum. Return to freezing unit and finish freezing. Makes 1½ quarts.

Caramel Ice Cream

2 cups sugar
1 cup hot water
1 quart milk
4 egg yolks
4 tablespoons sugar

½ teaspoon almond extract
1 cup chopped blanched almonds
2 cups heavy cream, whipped

Put 2 cups sugar in iron frying pan and heat slowly, stirring constantly, until the sugar is almost black. Very slowly add hot water and cook the syrup until the amount is slightly reduced (by about ¼ cup). In a saucepan heat milk to simmering point; then pour it gradually over egg yolks beaten with 4 tablespoons sugar. Return to fire and cook custard until it thickens. Add caramel syrup to the custard by teaspoonfuls until the custard is brown. Add almond extract and almonds. Mix thoroughly. Freeze partially in freezing tray. Then beat well, and fold in whipped cream. Complete freezing.

Fruit Sherbet

1 cup sugar	Juice of 3 oranges
1 cup water	Juice of 3 lemons
3 bananas	1 cup crushed pineapple

Boil sugar and water together for 5 minutes. Cool. Mash bananas with a fork, beat until creamy and add with all other ingredients to syrup. Blend well. Freeze in refrigerator tray. I consider this especially delicious.

Mississippi Mud

1 pint vanilla ice cream	1 pint bourbon
1 pint black coffee, very strong and cold	

Beat all together, preferably with an electric mixer. Sprinkle with grated nutmeg if desired. Serve.

Peach Ice Cream

2 cups peach pulp	½ teaspoon almond extract
¾ cup sugar	2 cups heavy cream
Pinch of salt	2 tablespoons sugar
Juice of 1 lemon	

Select soft ripe peaches; peel and put through a sieve. Add sugar, salt, lemon juice, and almond extract. When sugar is dissolved, pour into tray and freeze to a mush. Whip cream; add 2 tablespoons sugar and blend with peach mixture. Return to freezing tray. Stir once and finish freezing.

Plum Pudding (*Old English recipe*)

¼ pound shelled almonds,
    blanched
½ pound suet
1 cup stale bread crumbs
1 cup flour, sifted
1 cup sugar
½ teaspoon salt
4 eggs
1 wineglass (4 ounces) brandy

½ cup milk
½ teaspoon ground cloves
½ teaspoon grated nutmeg
½ teaspoon ground cinnamon
¼ pound candied orange peel
¼ pound candied lemon peel
½ pound seedless raisins
½ pound currants

Blanch, toast, and chop almonds. Chop suet fine and add bread crumbs. Then flour, sugar, salt; add well-beaten eggs, brandy, and milk. Add all other ingredients, blending well. Put in well-greased mold and steam, closely covered, for 5 or 6 hours. All that is needed for the steaming is a covered pudding mold (pound coffee can may be used), a deep covered kettle, and a rack on which to set the mold. Put the cover on the kettle, keep water (2 or 3″ deep) boiling gently for time specified.

Strawberry Shortcake

1 tablespoon butter
2 tablespoons sugar
1 egg
1 cup flour
1 teaspoon baking powder

¼ teaspoon salt
Strawberries
Sugar
Whipped cream (optional)

Beat butter until creamy. Add sugar gradually, beating after each addition. Add unbeaten egg and beat mixture thoroughly. Add flour sifted with baking powder and salt and blend well. Bake in 2 well-greased round cake pans in 325-degree oven about 20 minutes. Cap berries, mash slightly and mix with sugar to taste and spread between cake layers. Serve hot or cold with or without whipped cream.

Tutti-Frutti

This is a Christmas favorite dating back to colonial times and to be complete had to be started in the strawberry season and other fruits added as their season of the year rolled around.

1 quart apple brandy	1 pound sugar

Put these two items into 4 half-gallon jars or a 2-gallon crock. Keep covered with cloth tied on. Allow brandy and sugar to stand 1 week before any fruit is added. Add 1 pound of strawberries with ½ pound of sugar. Allow this in turn to stand one week before other fruit is added. As obtainable, add pineapple, white seedless grapes, cherries (pitted), and peaches, peeled and finely chopped. An interval of at least a week should elapse before a new fruit is added. Add 1 pound of fruit each time and always ½ pound of sugar at the same time. There should always be excess sugar in the bottom of the container or containers to prevent the fruits souring. Keep in a cool dark place for at least six weeks after the last fruit is added before using. Tutti-frutti should keep indefinitely. It was formerly used during the Christmas holidays as a topping for blanc-mange, boiled custard, or ice cream.

PIES

Apple Pie

2 cups applesauce (Made with tart spring apples, 4 or 5 required)	1 tablespoon butter, melted
	1 teaspoon lemon juice
1½ cups light brown sugar (about)	½ teaspoon nutmeg

Only apple pies made when green apples are in season seem worth the making or eating to me, but they can be delicious.

Peel and slice apples. Wash slices and put in a saucepan over moderate heat. Add about 1½ cups brown sugar, more or less to suit taste. Cook until apples have come to pieces. Add butter, lemon juice, and nutmeg and blend well. Put in uncooked pie shell. Cover with pastry thinly rolled. Prick with fork and press edges together with fork tines. Place in 350-degree oven and cook until crust is golden brown.

Damson Caramel Pie

The only answer I have been able to obtain as to why these pies are called caramel in Virginia is that our early colonists here were so fond of a caramel flavor that to obtain it they combined damson preserves with white sugar before brown sugar was available to them. This is really Chess Pie with preserves added.

4 eggs	1 cup damson preserves
1 cup sugar	½ cup butter, melted
Pinch of salt	1 teaspoon vanilla

Beat eggs together until light and foamy. Add sugar, salt, preserves, and melted butter, blending well. Add vanilla. Bake in uncooked pastry shell in two 8-inch pie plates. Less sugar may be used if a less sweet pie is desired, depending on tartness of preserves. This is my favorite pie with the possible exception of gooseberry, and gooseberries are rarely seen on the Richmond market.

Chess Cakes or Chess Pies

Out of the number of recipes I have for chess pies I selected the following as it is the one I have used most often. There are more opulent versions I know, some of them calling for entirely too much butter for the size of the pie.

5 tablespoons white corn meal	5 tablespoons milk
1⅔ cups sugar	1 tablespoon lemon or vanilla
Pinch of salt	extract
4 eggs	½ cup butter

Sift meal, sugar, and salt together and add well-beaten eggs. Add milk and flavoring. Heat butter to boiling point and pour over meal and egg mixture and stir until well blended. Put in an uncooked pastry shell and bake in 350-degree oven until filling has set and pastry is brown.

Although their origin is not definitely known, the designation Chess Cakes is believed to have been originally applied because of their convenience for use as refreshments at the chess table. While they are often baked nowadays in full-size pie plates, they were in earlier days more frequently baked in small individual tins. I am inclined to think from what some "old-timers" have told me, that they were originally called Cheese Cakes and the name was gradually changed to its present form after cheese was deleted from the recipe.

Cocoanut Pie

1 cup cocoanut
⅔ cup sherry
2 eggs, separated
Sugar to equal weight of cocoanut meat

Pinch of salt
⅓ teaspoon ground mace
2 teaspoons sugar
1 tablespoon lemon juice

Remove hull and brown skin from cocoanut meat and grate a sufficient quantity to make 1 cup. Pour sherry over this. Beat egg yolks with sugar and salt until very light. Add mace. Pour into one 8-inch pie plate lined with pastry. Bake until a delicate brown. Make meringue with egg whites to which 2 teaspoons sugar have been added. Season meringue with lemon juice. Spread over pies and return to oven to brown lightly.

Cream Pie

1 cup evaporated milk
3 eggs, separated
½ cup sugar
Pinch of salt
1 tablespoon gelatin
3 tablespoons cold water

1 teaspoon vanilla
¼ teaspoon nutmeg
½ pint (1 cup) heavy cream, whipped (sweetened to taste)
Grated chocolate

Scald milk. Beat egg yolks until thick and a pale yellow, adding sugar and salt. Beat scalded milk into egg yolk mixture and cook in double boiler until it reaches consistency of thick cream. Stir constantly. Remove from heat and add gelatin which has been softened in 3 tablespoons cold water for 5 minutes. Add vanilla and nutmeg. Cool. When mixture begins to thicken, beat with an egg beater and fold in stiffly beaten egg whites. Pour into a baked 9-inch pie shell and refrigerate until firm. Spread whipped cream on top and sprinkle with grated chocolate. Pie should stand several hours before being cut.

Lemon Meringue Pie

1 cup sugar
¼ cup flour
Pinch of salt
1 lemon, juice and grated rind
2 egg yolks, well beaten
1 tablespoonful butter

½ cup boiling water
½ cup milk
1 baked pastry shell
2 egg whites for meringue
2 tablespoonfuls sugar

Sift sugar and flour with salt. Add lemon juice and rind, egg yolks, butter, and boiling water. Cook in double boiler until mixture thickens, then add milk and cook a few minutes more. Cool. Pour into cooled baked pastry shell. Beat egg whites and 2 tablespoons sugar together. Spread over top of pie and brown in 350-degree oven.

Mince Meat for Mince Pies (*à la Queen Victoria*)

2 pounds suet
2 pounds apples
2 pounds seeded raisins
2 pounds currants
1 pound sultanas
¼ pound citron
¼ pound lemon peel
¼ pound orange peel

2 whole nutmegs, grated
1 teaspoon salt
1 teaspoon ginger
1 teaspoon allspice
1 teaspoon cloves (or less)
Juice and grated rind of 1 lemon
½ cup brandy
½ cup sherry

Use finely chopped suet from which all skin has been removed. Peel, core, and chop apples; chop other ingredients. Mix all together and put in stone crock (preferably), cover, and allow to ripen for about 6 weeks.

Pecan Pie

1 cup light brown sugar	1 cup milk, scalded
½ cup hot water	2 tablespoons butter
2 eggs	1 teaspoon vanilla
2 tablespoons flour	1 tablespoon rum
¼ teaspoon salt	Pecan halves

Boil brown sugar with hot water for about 5 minutes or until the mixture is a medium thick syrup. Cool. Beat eggs slightly and add sifted flour and salt, blending well. Scald milk in top of double boiler and add gradually to egg and flour mixture. Return to top of double boiler and cook over boiling water until it is about consistency of soft custard. Remove pan from heat and stir in butter, half of cooled brown sugar syrup, vanilla, and rum. Put filling in unbaked pie shell and cover with pecan halves. Pour other half of brown sugar syrup over pecans to make a glaze. Bake pie in 450-degree oven 15 or 20 minutes or until a golden brown.

Rum Cream Pie

6 egg yolks	1 pint (2 cups) heavy cream
1 cup sugar	½ cup rum
Pinch of salt	¼ cup strong black coffee
1½ envelopes gelatin	Sweet chocolate or pistachio nuts
½ cup cold water	

Gradually add sugar and salt to well-beaten egg yolks. Soak gelatin in water. Put gelatin and water over a low flame and stir until dissolved. Pour over egg and sugar mixture and stir briskly. Whip cream until stiff and fold into first mixture. Add rum and coffee. Refrigerate until mixture begins to set, then pour into baked pie shell. Return to refrigerator until firm. Sprinkle top of pie with shaved sweet chocolate or finely chopped pistachio nuts. Garnish edges of crust with whipped cream if desired.

Old Virginia Pie

Graham crackers (or zwieback)
  for crust
¼ cup sugar
⅓ cup of soft butter
15 marshmallows

Pinch of salt
½ cup milk
1 cup heavy cream, whipped
1 cup crushed peanut brittle
Shaved sweet chocolate

To make crust, use either ½ package (about) of graham crackers or zwieback. Roll into fine crumbs. Mix crumbs with ¼ cup sugar and ⅓ cup of soft butter. Line 9-inch pie pan with mixture and chill in refrigerator overnight to insure firm crust. Add marshmallows and salt to milk and melt over hot water. Cool and add whipped cream and peanut brittle. Pour into crust. Chill. Sprinkle top of pie with shaved chocolate.

Beverages

Café Nero

6 cubes sugar
8 Julienne strips lemon peel
8 Julienne strips orange peel
12 Julienne strips apple peel
12 cloves

½ stick cinnamon, broken into
  bits
6 ponies cognac
Black coffee

Into a chafing dish over a low flame place cubes of sugar, lemon and orange peel, apple peel, cloves, cinnamon, and cognac. When mixture is hot, saturate a sugar cube with the liquid, light with match and return it to mixture to set it afire. Allow it to burn, stirring constantly, for one minute; then while still burning, ladle it into after-dinner coffee cups which have been filled two-thirds full of strong black coffee. Serves 10.

153

Eggnog

This is the favorite eggnog of a former commander of a branch of our armed forces:

1 dozen eggs, separated	1 quart whiskey
1 pound confectioner's sugar	1 quart milk
1 quart light rum	1 quart whipping cream
6 ounces heavy rum	

Beat egg yolks until thick and pale yellow. Into yolks beat the pound of sugar. Add light rum slowly, beating all the while. Add heavy rum, whiskey, milk, and stiffly beaten cream. Fold in well-beaten egg whites. Leave eggnog on ice for 24 hours. Stir before serving and top with light sprinkling of nutmeg is desired. Serves about 60 people.

Eggnog, Martha

It's easy to see by the number of recipes given that eggnog is my favorite alcoholic drink and the following is my special favorite among them:

6 eggs, separated	½ wineglass white wine (about 3 ounces)
½ pound sugar	1 pint milk
1 pint apple brandy	1 pint whipping cream

Add sugar to well-beaten yolks. Into this mixture pour the brandy in a fine stream, beating at the same time. Stir in wine. Add milk next. Fold in stiffly beaten egg whites. Fold in cream which has been stiffly whipped. Pass nutmeg when serving. (I don't like nutmeg either in or on eggnog.) This quantity should serve 15, depending on the number of "seconds" requested.

Rush's Eggnog

18 eggs
½ pound sugar
2 quarts whiskey
1 pint California brandy
3 quarts whipping cream

20 teaspoons sugar
1 quart milk
2 jiggers rum
2 jiggers curaçao
Nutmeg

Separate egg whites and yolks. Beat yolks until thick. Put them into a two-gallon container. Add sugar until mixture pours off of spoon smoothly. Add whiskey and brandy by pouring in a slow, steady stream, stirring in one direction constantly. Do not whip. Add stiffly beaten cream slowly, stirring at the same time. If you like sweet eggnog, add 20 teaspoons of sugar to milk, stirring until dissolved. Add to eggnog. Then fold in three-fourths of stiffly beaten egg whites. Put the remainder of egg whites on top for decoration and sprinkle with grated nutmeg before serving. Add rum and curaçao just before serving to make the eggnog smooth. Serves approximately 60.

George Washington's Eggnog

1 pint brandy
½ pint rye whiskey
¼ pint Jamaica or New England
   rum
¼ pint sherry

12 eggs
12 tablespoons sugar
1 quart milk
1 quart whipping cream,
   whipped

Mix liquor first. Separate eggs. Beat yolks and add sugar. Mix well. Add liquor mixture slowly, beating constantly. Add milk, then whipped cream while slowly beating. Beat whites of eggs until stiff and fold slowly into mixture. Allow to stand in a cool place for several days. "Taste frequently" the directions conclude. Serves about 50.

Westmoreland Club Eggnog

The Westmoreland Club in Richmond, Virginia, has now passed out of existence. It was famous in its long day in the social life of Richmond.

36 eggs, whites and yolks beaten separately
36 tablespoons powdered sugar (plus 2 cups)

36 ounces of French brandy
8 ounces of rum
18 ounces of heavy cream

Add powdered sugar to beaten egg yolks and beat well. Then slowly beat in French brandy and rum. Next beat in stiffly beaten cream and lastly the beaten egg whites. Serves about 40.

Mint Julep (Southern)

1 teaspoon sugar
Water
Mint, 2 or 3 sprigs

Cracked ice
2 jiggers bourbon (3 ounces)
Mint

Use just enough water to dissolve sugar thoroughly. Add 2 or 3 tender sprigs of mint, not bruised. Fill cup (preferably metal) with finely cracked ice. Add bourbon and stir gently. Add a little more finely cracked ice and allow to stand until frosting takes place. Garnish with mint.

Mint Julep (Jersey)

1 teaspoon confectioner's sugar
Water
Crushed ice

Mint sprigs
Cognac
Peach brandy

Put sugar into a large glass. Add sufficient water to dissolve. Fill glass with crushed ice and sprigs of mint. Add cognac and peach brandy in equal proportions until liquid comes to top of glass. Stir gently.

Fairy Punch

¼ of a fresh pineapple cubed
1 quart unfermented grape
   juice, regular
1 cup cold tea
Juice of 3 oranges
1 lemon, sliced

½ banana, sliced
2 cups sugar
A few cherries
Ice
Carbonated water

Mix above ingredients and blend well. Place a small block of ice in a punch bowl and pour in above ingredients. When ready to serve, add more ice and 1 quart of carbonated water.

Tea Nog

¾ cup black tea
5 quarts boiling water
1 small box stick cinnamon
1 box whole cloves
¾ cup strained honey

1 orange rind
1 lemon rind
2 cups water
Juice of 3 oranges
Juice of 6 lemons

Make 5 quarts of strong tea using ¾ cup black tea to 5 quarts boiling water. Cook cinnamon sticks, cloves, honey, and orange and lemon rinds in 2 cups water for 10 minutes. Let stand an hour, then strain. Add orange and lemon juice and hot strong tea. Serve hot. These quantities will make 48 cups.

Tomato Juice Cocktail

6 ounces tomato juice
White pepper
Salt
Tabasco

1 teaspoonful dry sherry
Worcestershire sauce
Lemon wedges

Chill tomato juice and season to taste with white pepper, salt, and tabasco. When ready to serve, put a teaspoonful of good dry sherry and a few drops of Worcestershire sauce into each glass. Serve with lemon wedges.

Dandelion Wine

Water, boiling, 1 gallon
1 quart dandelions (blossoms and
   stems)
3 oranges (include rind)

3 lemons (include rind)
3 pounds sugar
½ yeast cake

Pour the boiling water over dandelions, sliced oranges, and lemons.
Allow to stand 3 days. Strain. Add sugar and yeast. Let stand 4 or
5 days. Then bottle and cork loosely until fermentation has stopped.
Then cork tightly and keep in cool, dark place until ready for use.
It's better to make it one year for the next.

Grape Wine

1 peck ripe grapes (preferably
   Concord)

1 quart boiling water
3 pounds sugar

Crush grapes and pour the boiling water over them. Allow to stand
36 to 48 hours, or until they begin to sing. Then squeeze through
fine cheesecloth (or muslin) and add sugar. Skim every morning
as long as scum rises. Strain again before bottling which should
be done in about 6 weeks.

Pickles and Relishes

Buck and Breck (*1 version, there are many*).
Sometimes called Cold Catsup or Tomato Relish
(*Uncooked*)

½ peck ripe tomatoes, peeled, cut
    fine and drained overnight
1 pint freshly grated horseradish
    (dehydrated mixed with
    water as directed on the
    bottle can be used if fresh
    not available)
¼ cup salt
1 cup mustard seed
2 sweet red peppers, finely
    chopped

2 sweet green peppers, finely
    chopped
5 stalks celery, finely chopped
1 cup onions (about 3 medium
    size) finely chopped
1 teaspoon ground cloves
2 teaspoons ground cinnamon
1 cup sugar
1 tablespoon black pepper
1 pint cider vinegar

Mix cold and put away cold. It is not necessary to seal although I usually do. It is necessary to use apple cider vinegar of standard strength. Ready for use in about 3 weeks.

Tomato Catsup (Cooked)

1 peck ripe tomatoes
3 sweet red peppers
4 medium-size onions
2½ tablespoons salt
2 cups sugar
1 tablespoon celery seed
2 teaspoons mustard seed
1 tablespoon whole allspice

1 pod hot red pepper
2 or 3 cups apple cider vinegar
2 tablespoons paprika (Must be for looks, red look, that is. It seems mostly tasteless to me, although I own up to liking highly seasoned foods.)

Wash and chop tomatoes, peppers, and onions. Simmer until soft. Press through a fine sieve. Cook juice rapidly until reduced to about one-half. Add salt, sugar, and spices (tied in a muslin bag) and boil until very thick. Add vinegar and paprika about 10 minutes before removing from heat. Pour into hot jars and seal at once.

Chili Sauce

8 pounds (½ peck) ripe tomatoes
1½ teaspoons whole allspice
1½ teaspoons whole cloves
2 sticks cinnamon
1 cup finely chopped onions

1½ cups finely chopped sweet red peppers
1½ cups finely chopped sweet green peppers
2 cups apple cider vinegar
1 cup sugar
3 tablespoons salt

Peel tomatoes and chop finely. Put spices in muslin bag and add to tomatoes along with onions and peppers. Boil (preferably in a porcelain kettle) until reduced to about half of original quantity. Remove spices. Add vinegar, sugar, and salt and continue to cook for about 10 minutes, stirring constantly. Pour into hot sterilized jars and seal at once.

English Chutney

3 green peppers, seeded
1 medium-size onion
12 firm, tart apples, peeled
1½ cups seeded raisins
1 tablespoon salt
3 cups apple cider vinegar

1½ cups sugar
1½ tablespoons ground ginger
1½ cups tart grape jelly
Juice of 3 lemons
Grated rind of 1 lemon

Chop peppers, onions, apples, raisins. Place all ingredients in large saucepan and simmer about 1 hour, or until quite thick. Turn into hot sterilized jars and seal. This makes about ½ gallon.

Peach Chutney

½ peck (8 lbs.) peaches (before peeling)
2 medium-size onions
1 clove garlic
1 cup seeded raisins
5 cups apple cider vinegar

¼ cup mustard seed
2 tablespoons ground ginger
1 pod hot red pepper
4 cups brown sugar
2 teaspoons salt
Juice and grated rind of 1 lemon

Chop peeled peaches, onions, garlic, and raisins. Add half of vinegar and cook until soft. Add balance of vinegar and all other ingredients. Cook until thick (about chili sauce consistency). Pour into hot sterilized jars and seal at once. Apples or plums may be substituted for peaches in this recipe and more sugar added if desired.

Green Tomato Pickle

½ peck (8 pounds) green tomatoes
6 medium-size onions
½ cup salt
1½ cups sugar
2 pods hot red pepper, cut into several pieces
1 tablespoon dry mustard
1 tablespoon mustard seed

1 tablespoon celery seed
1 tablespoon allspice ⎫
1 tablespoon pepper- ⎬ in cheese-
corns ⎭ cloth bag
1 tablespoon horseradish (grated if fresh, unmixed if dehydrated)
4 cups apple cider vinegar

Slice tomatoes and onions. Sprinkle with salt. Allow to stand overnight. Drain. Rinse. Boil sugar and seasonings with vinegar for 5 minutes. Cool slightly. Add tomatoes and onions and simmer 20 minutes. Remove seasonings in bag. Pack pickle into hot sterilized jars and seal at once.

Green Tomato Slices

Slice 4 pounds small green tomatoes ¼ inch thick. Make a solution of 2 cups of slaked lime in 4 gallons of water. Soak tomatoes 24 hours in this solution. Rinse well in at least 4 waters. Cook tomatoes about 45 minutes in the following syrup:

1 quart apple cider vinegar
1 tablespoon mixed pickling
  spices (in cheesecloth bag)

4 cups sugar
Salt to taste

Remove tomatoes from this syrup and cook liquid down to a thick syrup. Remove spices. Fill sterilized jars with tomato slices, pour hot syrup over them, and seal.

Peach Pickle

1 pint apple cider vinegar
4 cups sugar

2 tablespoons mixed pickling
  spices
Peaches, peeled, whole

Boil vinegar, sugar, and pickling spices (in cheesecloth bag), in a large bottom kettle (preferably porcelain). Add as many peaches as syrup will cover (about 14 medium size). Put top on kettle and boil until peaches are tender. Remove peaches to a large platter. Continue to boil syrup and seasonings until syrup begins to thicken. Put a small quantity of syrup in jar before adding peaches so they will not crush. Add syrup until peaches in jar are covered. Seal. I seldom see clingstone peaches on the market. They used to be specified in recipes for peach pickle. I really prefer freestones when firm as they are not tough as clingstones sometimes are.

Pear Pickle

5 pounds pears (when peeled)   3 pounds sugar
½ package mixed pickling spices   3 cups apple cider vinegar

Put peeled pears and pickling spices (in cheesecloth bag) in porcelain kettle. Cover pears with the sugar and allow to stand overnight or about 12 hours. The following day add vinegar and cook until pears are tender. Remove bag of pickling spices. Fill sterilized jars with pears and cover with syrup. Seal. I prefer seckel pears (small) which are left whole. If large pears are used, these may be halved or quartered.

Watermelon Rind Pickle

2 quarts prepared rind   1 tablespoon whole allspice
2 quarts lime or salt water   1 tablespoon whole cloves
4 to 6 cups sugar   1 stick cinnamon
1 quart water   1 tablespoon crushed ginger root
1 quart apple cider vinegar

Trim the meat from large pieces of thick, firm watermelon rind. Soak rind in lime water (1 tablespoon slaked lime to 1 quart water) 4 hours or soak overnight in salt water (4 tablespoons salt to 1 quart water). Lime water makes a crisper pickle. Drain, rinse, cover with clear water and boil 1½ hours. Cool, then cut into serving size pieces. Trim off green part of rind and discard. Measure white part. (This may be done at the time the pink meat is removed, but is easier to do after rind has been partly cooked.) Boil 2 cups sugar, 1 quart water, 1 cup vinegar and spices (in cheesecloth bag) 5 minutes. Add rind. Simmer 30 minutes. Let stand overnight. Add remaining sugar and vinegar and boil gently until syrup is almost as thick as honey and rind is clear. Remove bag of spices. Add boiling water if syrup becomes too thick before rind is tender and clear. Pack rind into hot jars; cover with syrup and seal at once.

Spiced Prunes

1 pound prunes, cooked,
   drained
½ cup prune juice
½ cup apple cider vinegar
½ cup sugar

2 sticks cinnamon
2 or 3 small pieces of ginger root
Grated rind of ½ an orange
A few blanched almonds

Into kettle put all ingredients except prunes and almonds. Bring to boiling point. Add drained prunes. Simmer gently for 10 minutes. Remove prunes to bowl. Increase heat, bring syrup to a boil and cook for 5 minutes; add almonds and pour over prunes. May be served hot or cold with sweet or sour cream if desired.

Jams and Jellies, Marmalades and Preserves

Citrus Marmalade

1 grapefruit	Water
1 lemon	Sugar
1 orange	

Remove the peel from the fruit and put it in a saucepan with water to cover. Bring the water to a boil. Simmer the peel for 45 minutes and drain. Repeat this process twice more. Then grind half the peel in a meat grinder and cut the other half into thin strips with scissors. Break fruit into segments and discard membrane and seeds. Combine fruit and peel and weigh. Cover fruit and peel with water equal in weight to the weight of the fruit and peel. Boil for about 1 hour. Measure fruit and liquid and add an equal quantity of sugar. Boil until syrup is like thick honey and amber in color, about 1 hour. I have worked out this recipe to produce the thick fruity marmalade I like. As given, it makes about 3 pints, a relatively small quantity compared to some recipes calling for much more water and sugar. If a thinner marmalade is desired and a greater quantity, add water equal in weight to 3 times the weight of the fruit and peel.

Damson Preserves (this recipe may also be used for all varieties of plums)

2 cups damsons   1½ cups sugar

Wash, drain, and remove seeds from damsons with sharp paring knife. Reserve some of the seeds and add to preserves in cheesecloth bag for flavor. Add sugar and allow to stand for several hours in crockery or in porcelain kettle in which preserves are to be cooked. Boil preserves briskly until syrup will jelly when small quantity is cooled. Remove bag of seeds. Pour preserves into hot sterilized jars and seal. Some people prefer to leave seeds in and skim out when preserves are done. The seeds do undoubtedly add to the characteristic flavor of damson preserves, but I prefer my damson preserves without the few seeds that seem to be inevitably left in by this method.

Kumquat Preserves

1 quart box kumquats   1 cup water
3 cups sugar   1½ cups light-colored rum

Boil sugar and water together for 5 minutes. Wash kumquats and dry. Drop in boiling syrup and cook gently for 45 minutes or until tender. Put fruit in hot sterilized jars, cook syrup down to half, add rum to hot syrup and pour over fruit until jar is full.

Pumpkin Jam

1 14- to 16-pound pumpkin, not too ripe
Sugar

5 teaspoons ground ginger
3 lemons, peel and juice

Remove seeds. Peel pumpkin and cut in 1½-inch cubes. Weigh pumpkin after it has been prepared and add ¾ pound of sugar for each pound of pumpkin. Let this mixture stand overnight in a large mixing bowl or enamel kettle. In the morning, add the ginger and cut-up pieces of lemon peel. Simmer very slowly all day long or until syrup is thick. Stir lemon juice into the jam about half an hour before removing it from the heat.

Rose Petal Jam

Cut rose petals in ¼-inch strips, discarding the tough base. To measure, pack tightly in a cup, but do not bruise. Cover 2 cups of cut petals with 2 cups of lukewarm water and simmer 10 minutes, or until tender. Lift petals out; make syrup with 1 cup of rose-petal liquid, 2⅔ cups sugar, and 2 tablespoons of strained honey. Cook to syrup stage or 220 degrees by candy thermometer. Add drained petals and simmer for 40 minutes. Add 1 teaspoon lemon juice and simmer 30 minutes longer. The color may be intensified by the addition of a bit of vegetable coloring if desired. Pour in sterile jars and seal at once. The honey is added for flavor and the lemon juice to keep petals tender. It is better to use an asbestos mat over very low heat as a very low temperature in cooking is essential.

Japonica Jelly

Collect quinces from japonica bush very late in the season, just before frost. Wash, cut in quarters, seeds and skin included. Cook until soft in sufficient water to cover. Then put fruit and remaining liquid in bag made of three thicknesses of cheesecloth. Suspend above a large kettle and allow to drip overnight. Next morning using equal quantities of sugar and juice boil rapidly until mixture jells when a drop is cooled, or for about 1 hour. Pour into sterile jars with screw tops or cover with paraffin in jelly glasses.

Brandied Peaches

Peaches, peeled   Water
Sugar   Brandy

Boil peaches in syrup made of 1 cup sugar and 1 cup of water for every pound of prepared fruit. Cook until tender, about 10 minutes. Place in crocks or wide-mouth glass jars, putting a small quantity of syrup and brandy in the container first to avoid crushing peaches when added. Mix syrup remaining after peaches are cooked with an equal quantity of brandy. Fill container with syrup-brandy mixture and cover tightly. Leave undisturbed for about 6 months (if you can).

Peach Preserves

2 pounds peaches, after skinning   2 cups water
   and pitting   3 cups sugar

Cut peeled peaches into halves. Boil sugar and water 2 minutes. Cool syrup. Add peaches and cook about 10 minutes or until tender. Let stand 4 hours. Lift peaches out and pack in hot jars. Boil syrup until thick as honey. Pour hot syrup over peaches to cover completely. Seal at once. If there is not sufficient syrup to cover peaches, make additional using 1 cup sugar to 1 cup water and boiling about 10 minutes.

Strawberry Preserves

2 quarts strawberries. Cover with boiling water and allow to stand 2 minutes. Put in colander and let all water run off. Put in kettle

and add 4 cups of sugar. Let come to hard boil and boil 5 minutes. Then add 2 more cups of sugar. Boil 5 minutes longer. Allow to stand overnight, put in jars when cold and seal.

Strawberry Preserves (*electric-light method and sunshine method*)

Wash and hull 1 quart strawberries. Place in colander; then stand in bowl and pour boiling water over them; drain immediately. Put strawberries in saucepan; add 1 cup sugar and boil moderately for 2 minutes. Add 2 cups sugar and boil 5 minutes longer. Skim. Pour into shallow glass or enamelware pan. Place under 100-watt electric light placed 6 to 10 inches away (gooseneck lamp is desirable). Cover lamp and preserves with a cloth. Allow to stand 36 to 48 hours, turning strawberries over every 6 or 8 hours until they are translucent and syrup is thick. Pack in sterilized jars and seal.
Follow same method for making strawberry preserves in the sun. Place pane of glass over flat pan of preserves and set in hot sunshine. Bring preserves inside at night and return to sunshine next day. I used electric light only during waking hours and I found about 25 hours sufficient for making quantity indicated (1 quart). As perhaps is often the case, the time I chose for the sunshine method was not particularly clear sunny weather. Under favorable conditions, either electric or sunshine method keeps berries whole and provides a nice thick syrup.

Confectioneries

Apple Candy

2 tablespoons powdered pectin
2 cups sugar
¼ cup corn syrup, light
Pinch of salt

2 tablespoons cornstarch
1¼ cups apple juice
Powdered sugar

Mix pectin with 1 tablespoon of the sugar and blend well with corn syrup. Blend cornstarch with ¼ cup apple juice. Bring remaining apple juice to a boil and pour over mixture of pectin, sugar, syrup, and salt. Heat slowly for 2 minutes, stirring constantly to prevent sticking. Add apple juice-cornstarch mixture. Heat for 2 more minutes, stirring constantly. Add remaining sugar to this mixture and blend well. Slowly heat, with constant stirring for 10 minutes. Pour into enameled pan. Refrigerate until stiff enough to cut into squares. Then roll in powdered sugar.

Candied Orange, Lemon and Grapefruit Peel

Remove pulp from fruit and cut peel in strips of desired size; soak orange and lemon peel overnight in cold water but let grapefruit rind soak in salt water overnight (1 tablespoon salt to 1 quart of water). Use separate utensils for each fruit (enamel or preferably crockery). Next morning cover drained peel with fresh water and bring slowly to a boil. Lemon and grapefruit peel should come to a boil 3 times in cold water, the old water being discarded each time after 30 minutes of boiling. Orange peel needs only 1 change. In the last water boil until the rind is tender, about 30 minutes. Drain thoroughly and measure the rind. Take equal quantities of sugar and rind and half as much water. Cover and let stand overnight. Bring to a boil and cook until clear, about 1 hour. Spread out to dry, first rolling each piece well in granulated sugar.

Martha Washington Butter Creams

¼ pound butter
1 pound XXXX sugar
1 teaspoon vanilla

Pinch of salt
4 squares unsweetened chocolate
1 tablespoon paraffin

Cream butter; sift sugar and beat into butter until light. Add vanilla and salt. Store in refrigerator for 12 hours. Shape into desired forms adding nut meats or crystallized fruits if desired, and dip in the chocolate and paraffin which have been melted together over boiling water. (Not on direct heat as paraffin is inflammable.) After dipping creams into mixture, set on buttered platter to harden.

Chocolate Cream Fudge

1 tablespoon butter
1 cup light brown sugar
1 cup granulated sugar
½ cup sweet milk

½ cup sour cream
½ teaspoon salt
3 squares unsweetened chocolate
1 teaspoon vanilla

Butter heavy aluminum 1-gallon saucepan with the butter. Add sugar, milk, sour cream, and salt. Cook over very low heat until sugar is dissolved, stirring occasionally. Then cook briskly, stirring only occasionally to keep from sticking, until candy forms soft ball in cool water. Remove pan from stove and add chocolate which has been cut into very small pieces. As soon as chocolate melts, set pan in sink or large pan of cold water for 5 minutes. Remove pan from cold water and beat with a large kitchen spoon until fudge becomes creamy. Add vanilla and stir slowly until fudge is very thick. Pour out in buttered pan. Cut in squares when sufficiently hard.

Chocolate Fudge (*my method*)

2 cups sugar
1 cup milk
Pinch of salt

1 square unsweetened chocolate
1 teaspoon butter
1 teaspoon vanilla

Put sugar, milk, salt, and the chocolate just as it comes from the wrapper in a saucepan (preferably heavy) and place over very low heat until sugar and chocolate are thoroughly dissolved. Then cook quickly until the mixture forms a soft ball in cool water, stirring occasionally from the bottom to prevent sticking. Remove from heat and cool until about lukewarm. Add butter and vanilla and begin beating. Continue beating until it begins to stiffen. Pour out in buttered pan and cut into squares when it has hardened sufficiently. This proportion of chocolate and sugar gives a rather sweet fudge.

Cocoanut Cream Candy

2 teaspoons butter
1½ cups sugar
Pinch of salt

½ cup milk
⅓ cup fresh grated cocoanut
½ teaspoon vanilla

Put butter into saucepan (preferably heavy) and, when melted, add sugar, salt, and milk. Keep heat very low until sugar is dissolved, stirring occasionally. Increase heat and boil briskly for 10 minutes. Remove from heat and add cocoanut and vanilla. Allow to cool slightly. Beat until creamy and mixture begins to thicken.

Pour into buttered pan and cut in squares when candy is hard. One-half cup of nutmeats (broken or cut into small pieces) may be substituted for the cocoanut.

Cream Mints (Uncooked)

2 tablespoons butter
2 tablespoons vegetable fat
Pinch of salt

2 cups warm water
2 cups sifted XXXX sugar

Cream butter, vegetable fat, and salt. (Satisfactory results cannot be obtained unless both butter and vegetable fat are used.) Add warm water. Beat until creamy. Flavor and color as desired (5 drops of mint or peppermint and pink, yellow or green vegetable coloring). Add sugar gradually and blend well into creamed mixture until a roll can be formed. Wrap roll in wax paper. Chill until hard enough to slice for serving. Makes 24 mints.

Divinity Fudge

2¼ cups sugar
⅔ cup light corn syrup
¼ teaspoon salt
½ cup water

2 egg whites
1 teaspoon vanilla
1 cup finely chopped walnut
meats

Put sugar, syrup, salt, and water into a saucepan. Stir over low heat until sugar has dissolved. Then cook without stirring until mixture forms hard ball in cool water. Pour hot syrup slowly into stiffly beaten egg whites, beating constantly. Beat until candy will hold its shape when dropped from spoon. Add vanilla and nut meats. Drop by teaspoonfuls onto waxed paper or pour into buttered pan and mark off in squares when candy has hardened sufficiently.

Panocha

1 cup sugar
1 cup light brown sugar
½ cup coffee cream
2 tablespoons dark corn syrup

1 tablespoon butter
2 tablespoons water
Pinch of salt
¾ cup finely chopped nut meats

Cook all ingredients except nut meats together over low heat. Continue cooking for 5 minutes after boiling point is reached. Remove from heat. Beat thoroughly and add the nut meats. Pour into buttered pan and mark into squares before candy hardens completely.

Sherried Pecan Pralines

1 cup light brown sugar
1 cup granulated sugar
¼ cup coffee cream
¼ cup sherry

Pinch of salt
3 tablespoons butter
1½ cups pecan halves

Combine brown sugar, granulated sugar, cream, sherry, and salt, in a heavy saucepan. Place over low heat until sugar is dissolved; then cook, stirring occasionally, until a small quantity forms a very soft ball in cool water. (230 degrees on a candy thermometer.) Add butter and pecans; continue cooking to soft-ball stage (235 degrees), stirring frequently. Remove from heat and let stand 5 minutes; then stir until mixture is slightly thickened and looks cloudy. Drop by tablespoonful onto a buttered baking sheet to cool. Makes 12 pralines.

Sea Foam

3 cups light brown sugar
¼ teaspoon salt
¾ cup water

2 egg whites
1 teaspoon vanilla

Dissolve sugar and salt in water. Cook without stirring to hard-ball stage when small quantity is dropped in cool water. Remove from heat and pour gradually over stiffly beaten egg whites, beating constantly. Add vanilla. Continue beating until candy cools and will hold its shape. Then drop by teaspoonfuls onto waxed paper, or spread into buttered pan and mark in squares.

Index

Appetizers

Bacon Biscuit Balls, 3
Beets, Stuffed, 4
Butter Browns, 4
Calcuttas, 4
Canapé Spread, 4
Celery Cheese Balls, 5
Cheese Apples, 5
Cheese Biscuits, 5–6
Cheese Diamonds, 6
Cheese Snappies, 6
Cheese Spread, 6–7
Chicken and Celery Spread, 7
Chicken Balls, 7
Chicken Liver Paste, 7
Clam Dip, 8
Cocktail Crackers, 8
Crab Meat Canapé, 8
Cucumber Finger Sandwiches, 9

Appetizers (continued)

Cucumber Slices, 9
Deviled Pecans, 11
Fresh Grapefruit Dip, 9
Guacamole, 10
Ham Pops, 10
Liver Paste Canapés, 10–11
Potato Chip Mixture, 11
Roll-ups, 11–12
Roquefort Cheese Canapé, 12
Roquefort Dip, 12
Seed Snacks, 12–13
Shrimp Dip, 13
Smoky Cheese Dip, 13
Texas Toasts, 13

Beverages

Café Nero, 153
Dandelion Wine, 158

179

Beverages (*continued*)
Eggnog, 154
Eggnog, Martha, 154
Fairy Punch, 157
George Washington's Eggnog, 155
Grape Wine, 158
Mint Julep (Jersey), 156
Mint Julep (Southern), 156
Rush's Eggnog, 155
Tea Nog, 157
Tomato Juice Cocktail, 157
Westmoreland Club Eggnog, 155

Breads (*Quick*)

Batter Bread, 17–18
Beaten Biscuits, 19–20
Blueberry Griddle Cakes, 22–23
Buttermilk Biscuits, 20
Buttermilk Waffles, 25–26
Chicken Crackling Biscuits, 21
Corn Sticks or Muffins, 19
Corn-Meal Griddle Cakes, 22
Corn-Meal Mush, 24
Crackling Corn Bread, 19
Griddle Cakes, 22
Huckleberry Muffins, 23
Hush Puppies, 25
Orange Nut Bread, 21
Plain Muffins, 23–24
Plantation Spoon Bread, 18
Popovers, 25
Popovers (Unbeaten), 24–25
Potato Pancakes, 23
Spoon Bread, 18
Sour Cream Muffins, 24

Breads (*Yeast*)

Bread, 28–29
Bread (with eggs and potatoes), 28
Buckwheat Cakes, 34
Buttermilk Rolls, 34–35
Flannel Cakes, 31
Homemade Loaf Bread, Toasted, 29

Breads (*Yeast*) (*continued*)
100-per-cent Whole-Wheat Bread, 33–34
Raised Muffins, 33
Rich Loaf Bread, 29
Rolls, 35
Sally Lunn, 31–32
Sally Lunn (with potato), 32
Salt Risen Bread, 29–30
Salt Risen Bread (with egg), 30–31
Southern Split Biscuits, 27–28

Cakes

Angel Food Cake, 117–118
Burnt-Almond Cake, 118–119
Burnt-Sugar Cake, 119
Burnt-Sugar Frosting, 119
Caramel Cake, 120
Caramel Nut Frosting, 120
Cheese Cake, Martha's, 120–121
Cocoanut Cake, 122
Dark Fruit Cake, 122–123
Devil's Food Cake, 123–124
Lane Cake, 125
Nut Cake, 126
Nut and Fruit Cake, 126–127
Pound Cake, 127
Robert E. Lee Cake, 125–126
Rocky Mountain Cake, 127–128
Rum Cake, 128–129
Southern Belle Cake, 130–131
Tipsy Cake, 129
White Fruit Cake, 124–125
White Layer Cake, 130

Cake Frostings (*Cooked*)

Divinity Frosting, 131
Egg Yolk Frosting, 131
Lemon Frosting, 132
7-Minute Frosting, 132

Cake Frostings (*Uncooked*)

Butter Frosting, 132
Chocolate Frosting, 133

Cake Frostings (Uncooked) (cont.)
Lemon Frosting, 133
Water Frosting, 133

Confectioneries

Apple Candy, 171
Candied Orange, Lemon and Grapefruit Peel, 172
Chocolate Cream Fudge, 172–173
Chocolate Fudge (my method), 173
Cocoanut Cream Candy, 173–174
Cream Mints, 174
Divinity Fudge, 174
Martha Washington Butter Creams, 172
Panocha, 174–175
Sherried Pecan Pralines, 175
Sea Foam, 175

Cookies

Brown Sugar Cookies, 134
Cocoanut Dream Bars, 134
Hazlenut Cookies, 135
Orange Crisps, 135
Shortbread Cookies, 136

Desserts

Bing Cherry Ice Cream, 144
Boiled Custard, 139–140
Caramel Ice Cream, 144
Cashew Dessert, 137–138
Crême Brulée, 138
Dulcet Cream, 138–139
Fried Cream, Flambé, 139
Frosted Grapes, 141
Fruit Sherbet, 145
Gingerbread, 140–141
Lemon Butter, 138
Maids of Honor, 141
Meringue Shells, 141–142
Mississippi Mud, 145
Old English Trifle, 142
Oranges (Cooked), 142
Peach Cobbler, 143
Peach Ice Cream, 145

Desserts (continued)
Peaches Celestial, 143
Persimmon Pudding, 143
Plum Pudding, 146
Strawberry Shortcake, 146
Tutti-Frutti, 147

Egg and Cheese Dishes

Buckingham Eggs, 77
Deviled Eggs and Mushrooms, 78
Eggs à la King, 78
French Fried Deviled Eggs, 79
Gay Nineties Rarebit, 80
Omelet, Plain, 79
Onion-Cheese Pasty, 80
Rancher's Omelet, 81
Welsh Rarebit with Ale, 81

Jams and Jellies, Marmalades and Preserves

Brandied Peaches, 168
Citrus Marmalade, 165–166
Damson Preserves, 166
Japonica Jelly, 167–168
Kumquat Preserves, 166–167
Peach Preserves, 168
Pumpkin Jam, 167
Rose Petal Jam, 167
Strawberry Preserves, 168–169
Strawberry Preserves (Electric Light and Sunshine Method), 169

Meats

Applesauce Apples, 57
Baked Ham Loaf, 58
Baked Ham Slice, 55
Bewitched Liver, 60–61
Chili Con Carne, 51
Cooking Country Ham with Blanket, 52
Country Ham (cooked with "Spirits"), 54
Country Ham (with blanket made of yeast dough), 52–53

Meats (*continued*)
Filet Mignon with Maître d'Hôtel Butter, 50
Fried Country Ham, 54–55
Ham Cooked in Coca-Cola or Ginger Ale, 54
Ham Cooked in Wine, 55
Ham (ready to cook), 56
Ham Toppings, 56–57
Ham ("very old recipe"), 55–56
Hamburgers de Luxe, 46–47
High-Protein Meat Loaf, 48
Hog Jowl and Turnip Greens, 57
Individual Ham Loaves, 58
Irish Beef Pasties, 47
Jellied Meat Loaf, 48
Liver Loaf, 62
Liver Steaks French Fried, 62
Meat Loaf (by Martha), 48–49
Oxtails in Wine, 63
Pork Chops Baked in Sour Cream, 58–59
Pork Chops in Vermouth, 59–60
Roast Beef, 46
Roast Lamb, 60
Salt Pork and Fried Apples, 59
Salt Pork de Luxe, 59
Sausage Loaf, 61
Savory Pork Chops, 60
Smithfield Ham, 53
Steak Butter, 49–50
Stuffed Meat Loaf, 49
Stuffed Roast Beef, 45–46
Swiss Steak, 50–51
Spare Ribs, Barbecued, 61–62
Veal Casserole, 63
Veal Cutlet Provençal, 64
Veal Paprika, 64
Veal, Swiss, 64–65
Yorkshire Steak, 50

Pickles and Relishes

Buck and Breck, 159–160
Chili Sauce, 160
English Chutney, 161

Pickles and Relishes (*continued*)
Green Tomato Pickle, 161–162
Green Tomato Slices, 162
Peach Chutney, 161
Peach Pickle, 162
Pear Pickle, 163
Spiced Prunes, 164
Tomato Catsup, 160
Watermelon Rind Pickle, 163

Pies

Apple Pie, 147–148
Caramel Pie, 148
Chess Cakes or Chess Pies, 148–149
Cocoanut Pie, 149
Cream Pie, 149–150
Lemon Meringue Pie, 150
Mince Meat for Mince Pies, 150–151
Old Virginia Pie, 152
Pecan Pie, 151
Rum Cream Pie, 151

Poultry

Barbecued Chicken, 65
Broiled Chicken, 65–66
Chicken Country Captain, 66
Chicken Croquettes, 66–67
Chicken Livers, 69
Chicken Pie, 69–70
Chicken Pudding, 68–69
Chicken Scrapple, 70–71
Fried Chicken, 67
Jellied Chicken, à la King, 68
Old Fashion Roast Chicken, à la Martha, 70
Oven-Fried Chicken, 67
Roast Goose, 71
Roast Turkey, 71–72

Poultry Dressing and Dumplings

Chestnut Dressing, 72
Chestnut Dressing (with ham), 72

Poultry Dressing (continued)
Corn-Bread Dressing, 73
Corn-Meal Dumplings, 75
Drop Dumplings, 76
Ham and Nut Dressing for Roast Chicken, 73
Poultry Dressing (with Brazil nuts), 73–74
Poultry Dressing (with corn), 74
Typical Poultry Dressing, 74–75
Wild Rice Dressing, 75

Salads and Salad Dressings

Boiled Salad Dressing, 111–112
Chicken Salad, 107–108
Combination Salad, 108
Fruit Salad, 108–109
Lulu Paste, 109
Mayonnaise, 111
Onion-Orange Salad, 109
Potato Salad, 109–110
Salad Dressing (Uncooked), 112
Snap Bean Salad, 110
Waldorf Salad Jelly, 110
Water Cress Salad, 111

Sandwiches

Avocado-Cucumber Sandwiches, 15
Chicken Giblet Spread for Sandwiches, 15
Cream Cheese and Chili Sauce for Sandwiches, 16
Mushroom-Onion Sandwiches, 16

Sauces

Barbecue Sauce for Steak, 112
Brandy Sauce for Ham, 112
Cocktail Sauce, 113
Cranberry Sauce, 113
Cream Sauce, 113
Creamed Chicken Sauce, 114
Fruit Fritter Sauce, 114
Hollandaise Sauce, 114–115
Hollandaise Sauce (newer method), 115

Sauces (continued)
Horseradish Sauce, 115
Tomato Sauce, 115
White Sauce, 116
Wine Sauce, 116

Sea Foods

Baked Seafood au Gratin, 86–87
Baked Shad with Roe Stuffing, 88
Crab Cutlets, 83–84
Crab Meat on Wild Rice, 85
Deviled Oysters on Half Shell, 85–86
Oyster Sausage, 85
Scalloped Oysters, 86
Sea Food Newburg, 87
Shad Roe, 87
Shad Roe au Gratin, 88
Steamed Shrimp, 88–89
Stuffed Crabs, à la Creole, 84

Soup

Brunswick Soup, 37–38
Clam Chowder, 38
Cream of Chestnut Soup, 39
Fruit Soup, 40
Gumbo Filé, 40–41
Mrs. George Washington's Crab Soup, 39
Onion Soup, 41
Orange Soup, 41
Peanut Soup, 42
Potato and Avocado Soup, 42
Soup with Meat Balls, 42–43
Vichyssoise, 43
White Soup, 43

Vegetables

Baked Sweet Potatoes and Pippins, 103
Baked Bananas, 91
Beets in Orange Sauce, 92
Boston Baked Beans, 92
Broccoli Bake, 92–93
Broccoli with Parmesan Cheese, 93

Vegetables (*continued*)
Brussels Sprouts with Chestnuts, 93
Carrot Balls, 94
Cauliflower au Gratin, 94
Cauliflower in Pimiento Cups, 94–95
Celery Hearts Fried, 95–96
Chestnut Croquettes, 95
Chestnuts en Casserole, 95
Corn Pudding, 96
Corn Pudding Rosette, 96
Cucumbers Baked, 97
Cucumbers French Fried, 97
Eggplant High Hat, 97–98
Eggplant Medley, 98
Eggplant Stuffed, 98–99
French Fried Onions, 99
French Fried Rice, 103

Vegetables (*continued*)
Hopping John, 99
New Potatoes in Sauce, 102
Onions Stuffed, 100
Peanuts Baked, 100
Peas Epicurean, 101
Potato Apples, 101–102
Scalloped Potatoes, 102
Sliced Potatoes, 102
Snaps, 104
Sour Cream Cabbage, 93–94
Texas Stuffed Tomatoes, 104–105
Vegetable Casserole, 105
Wax Beans au Gratin, 105
Welsh Rabbit Peppers, 101
Wild Rice Croquettes, 103
Wild Rice with Chicken Livers, 104
Zucchini, 105–106